Academic Writing for Graduate Students

Hang around — stay   boot Camp → basic training

evaluative adj
adj in context
scare Quotes
p~2.
critical review Formula

informed & organized — summary
argumentative & evaluative — critique

Grammar for smart people   _Barri Tarshis_

content, composition

Academic Writing for Graduate Students

Essential Tasks and Skills

A Course for Nonnative Speakers of English

John M. Swales and Christine B. Feak

 MICHIGAN SERIES IN ENGLISH FOR
ACADEMIC & PROFESSIONAL PURPOSES

Series Editors: Carolyn G. Madden and John M. Swales
Advisor to the Series: Ann M. Johns

Ann Arbor

THE UNIVERSITY OF MICHIGAN PRESS

syllabication _"stress"_

"The ə"

Acknowledgments

Grateful acknowledgment is given to the following for use of copyrighted or manuscript material.

AIAA for "High Angle-of-Attack Calculations of the Subsonic Vortex Flow in Slender Bodies," by D. Almosino, *AIAA Journal* 23, no. 8, 1985.

Benny Bechor for "Navigation."

Jo-Ching Chen for her critique of "ESL Spelling Errors."

Horace H. Rackham School of Graduate Studies, University of Michigan, for "Years to Doctorate for Doctoral Programs at University of Michigan, Ann Arbor, for Students Entering in 1981–83."

Kazuo Ichijo for "Speed and Innovation in Cross-functional Teams."

IEEE for "Causes of PC Virus Infection in U.S. Businesses," by John B. Bowles and Colon E. Pelaez, in "Bad Code," *IEEE Spectrum*, August 1992.

Indiana University Press for adapted excerpts from *Conversational Joking*, by Neal R. Norrick, copyright © 1993.

Yasufumi Iseki for "Reducing Air Pollution in Urban Areas: The Role of Urban Planners."

Tiina Koivisto for "Rhythm, Meter and the Notated Meter in Webern's Variations for Piano, Op. 27."

Jiyoung Lee for "Comparison of the Actual CO_2 Levels with the Model Predictions."

Abdul Malik for his textual outline.

Pierre Martin for his textual outline.

Newsweek for source material from "Reaping the Clouds of Chile" by Mac Margolis, Newsweek Focus, *Newsweek*, October 18, 1993.

Oxford University Press for material adapted from *The Birds of Egypt*, edited by Steven Goodman, Peter Meininger, et al., copyright © 1989.

Physical Review for "Nuclear-Structure Correction to the Lamb Shift," by K. Pachucki, D. Leibfried, and T. W. Hänsch, *Physical Review A*, 48, no.1, July 1993.

Scientific American for source material for summary based on information from "Madagascar's Lemurs," by Ian Tattersall, *Scientific American*, January 1993.

Koji Suzuki for "Global Implications of Patent Law Variation."

Lee Tesdell for "ESL Spelling Errors," *TESOL Quarterly* 18, no. 2, 1984.

TESOL for "Chinese EFL Student's Learning Strategies for Oral Communication," by Huang Xiao-Hua, *TESOL Quarterly* 19, no. 1, 1985; and for material adapted from "Rhetorical Patterns in English and Chinese," by Hiroe Kobayashi, *TESOL Quarterly* 18, no. 4, 1984.

Jun Yang for "Binding Assay and Down Regulation Study."

Contents

Appendixes

Selected References   247

Introduction

Overview

- This textbook is designed to help graduate students with their *academic* writing.
- It is designed for nonnative speakers of English.
- It has evolved out of both research and teaching experience.
- The general approach is rhetorical; that is, it focuses on making a good impression with academic writing.
- The book is as much concerned with developing academic writers as it is with improving academic *texts*.
- The tasks, activities, and discussions are richly varied, ranging from small-scale language points to studying the discourse of a chosen discipline.
- The book is fast paced, opening with a basic orientation and closing with writing an article for publication.
- With the help of the accompanying commentary, students and scholars should be able to use this volume profitably on their own.

Audience

We have created this textbook for people who are not native speakers of English yet are studying for graduate degrees (at both masters and doctoral levels) through or partly through the medium of English. Although the book is primarily based on our experience at research universities in the United States, we believe that much of it will prove helpful and useful to graduate students in other countries. Parts of the book may also be of assistance to nonnative speaker scholars and researchers, particularly Units Seven and Eight, which deal with constructing a research paper for possible publication. By and large, we do not think *Academic Writing for Graduate Students* should be used with undergraduates, particularly those in their first year. In our experience, the strengths and weaknesses in the writing of nonnative speaker undergraduates and graduates are very different.

Origins

Academic Writing for Graduate Students (henceforth *AWG*) evolved out of our experiences over several years in teaching writing at the University of Michigan's English Language Institute, in particular, out of our experiences in ELI 320 (Academic Writing I), ELI 321 (Academic Writing II), and ELI 520 (Research Paper Writing). We have also done our best to incorporate into the teaching materials insights and findings derived from the growing number of studies into the characteristics of academic English itself. We are, in fact, firmly committed to the view that a book on academic English should itself be "academic," that is, not merely based on guesswork, untested speculation, and received opinion.

Restrictions

We know, of course, that academic English is a complex and unstable target. Especially at the graduate level, there are clear differences among texts typical of the arts (or humanities), the social sciences, the natural sciences, the life sciences, and those produced in professional schools such as engineering or architecture. For reasons that we will explain later, we nevertheless believe that this textbook will have something useful to say and teach about writing in much—but not all—of this very broad area. We would, in fact, only definitely exclude students who are following graduate degree courses in fields where the "essayist" tradition still prevails, such as in literature, or students whose writing requirements are professional (for example, persuasive memos in business administration, briefs in law, or case reports in medical sciences). We should perhaps also exclude graduate-level written work in mathematics, because of the unusual nature of such texts.

Rationale

By adopting the following strategies, we have tried to produce a book that will serve the needs of the remaining broad range of disciplines. First, for illustration, analysis, and revision, we have used texts drawn from this wide range of disciplines—from mechanical engineering to music theory. Second, we have stressed throughout that academic writing is rhetorical. All of us, as academic writers and whatever our backgrounds, are engaged with thinking about our readers' likely expectations and reactions, with deciding on what to say—and what not to say—about our data, and with organizing our texts in ways that meet local conventions and yet create a space for ourselves. Third, and perhaps most important, we have avoided laying down rules about what a member of a disciplinary community should (or should not) do in a particular writing situation. Instead, we have encouraged users of *AWG* to find out for themselves what the conventions of their fields actually are. For example, whether introductions to research papers should (or should not) include a summary of the principal results seems to vary among the disciplines; therefore, we ask users of the book to examine a small sample of introductions from their own fields and report back.

It is our experience, especially with more senior students, that a multidisciplinary class has several advantages over a monodisciplinary one. It turns attention away from whether the information or content in a student draft is "correct" toward questions of rhetoric and language. It thus encourages rhetorical consciousness. It leads to interesting group discussion among members from very different parts of the university. It can also create a special community of its own, especially since students are not directly competing with each other.

Throughout the book, we have stressed the concept of "positioning." In other words, we ask students to assess what they are writing in terms of how well it is positioning them as junior members of their chosen academic communities. To this end, we ask students to examine and discuss texts that some of our own students have written.

Organization

AWG is organized into eight units. The first three units are essentially preparatory; they prepare the way for the more genre-specific activities in later units. Unit One presents an overview of the considerations involved in successful academic writing, with a deliberate stress on early exposure to the concept of positioning. Units Two and Three deal with two overarching patterns in English expository prose: the movement from general to specific and the movement from problem to solution. Unit Four acts as a crucial link between the earlier and later units, since it deals with how to handle the discussion of data. Units Five and Six deal with writing summaries and critiques respectively. As might be expected, these two units require students to do more reading than the others. Finally, Units Seven and Eight deal with constructing a real research paper, that is, one that might be submitted for publication. As part of the last two units, we discuss the evolution of a potential small research paper of our own as an illustration of the research paper writing process.

There are also three Appendixes. Appendix One is a rapid review of article usage in academic English. Appendix Two aids reading as much as writing, since it provides a glossary of Latin terms still used in scholarly writing. Appendix Three deals with usage and "positioning" in E-mail communications.

Viewed as a whole, *AWG* is a fairly fast-paced course taking non-native speaker (NNS) graduate students from a basic orientation through to aiming at publication. We have opted for this approach because we suspect that most NNS graduate students will have only one opportunity to take a graduate writing course. At Michigan, however, the ELI currently offers a series of four, short 20-hour a semester writing courses. In such circumstances, there is sufficient depth and breadth of material in *AWG* to cover more than one course. This may be possible in other institutions as they expand their course offerings.

Language Review

We have stressed up until now the "rhetorical" or "strategic" approach we have adopted for *AWG*, an approach that is fleshed out through a task-based methodology. However, this does not mean that the surface features of grammar and phraseology (or, indeed, punctuation) have been ignored. Each unit typically contains two or three Language Focus sections that step away from rhetoric in order to deal with some linguistic feature. We have done our best to situate this linguistic work in an appropriate context. For example, part of Unit Two deals with definitions, and it is here that we discuss the grammar of reduced relative clauses, since these clauses are an integral part of such statements.

The Data in the Tables and Figures

There are 27 tables and 11 figures in the text. In some cases, the data in the nonverbal material is fully authentic. In some others, we have simplified, adapted, or reconfigured the data to make the associated writing task more "manageable." In these cases, the title of the table or figure is followed by a @@@.

Instructor Roles and the Commentary

We now turn to the issue of instructor role. We recognize that most instructors using this book will likely be experienced teachers of academic writing. Courses in graduate writing are not typically taught by new recruits to the English as a second language profession, by occasional part-timers, or by graduate students themselves. Experienced English for Academic Purposes instructors always need convincing that adopting a textbook is a better alternative than using their own materials. For that reason, we have aimed for a textbook that can be used selectively and that easily allows teachers to substitute activities and texts more suited to their own particular circumstances. In effect, we look on the instructor more as a partner in an educational enterprise than as the consumer of a textbook product.

In the same light, we do not wish to impose our own ideas (which are by no means identical in every case) about how *AWG* should actually be taught. We have nothing to say, for example, about the pros and cons of peer feedback, about the importance of revising, about the exchange of personal experience, or indeed about how to integrate the best of process and product approaches to writing. In consequence, no traditional teacher's handbook accompanies this text. Instead, we have provided a small companion volume entitled *Commentary*. This volume—which includes synopses of each unit, further discussion of points raised, suggestions for other work, and model answers to the more controlled tasks—can also serve as a self-study manual for students or scholars using *AWG* without the benefit of an instructor.

Collaboration and Assistance

Finally, we turn to all those who have helped us. Writing this textbook has incurred many debts. There are a number of people who, in general terms, have influenced our thinking about academic writing. Here we would like to specifically recognize the influence of Deborah Campbell, David Charles, Tony Dudley-Evans, Ann Johns, Marilyn Martin, and Ray Williams. We are also very grateful to the following for their useful comments on various drafts of various units: Ummul Ahmad, Diane Belcher, Barbara Dobson, Peggy Goetz, Ilona Leki, Margaret Luebs, Susan Reinhart, Theresa Rohlck, and Larry Selinker. We thank Cynthia Hudgins, who provided valuable administrative assistance in the initial stages of putting this book together. We owe a special debt to Peter Master for his close and perceptive reading of the entire final draft. We also thank Elizabeth Axelson, Kirstin Fredrickson, and Carolyn Madden for their help in field-testing the materials. Then there are all our students whose successes and failures with academic discourse have helped shape this text.

Throughout, we have much appreciated the steady encouragement provided by Mary Erwin of the University of Michigan Press. We are also grateful to the English Language Institute for providing the release time that has made this book possible. Finally, there are more personal debts. John is very grateful to Vi Benner for (yet again) supporting the untidy and distracting process of writing a book in a small house. Chris is very thankful for the encouragement of her colleague Sarah Briggs during the time she needed it most. She is also grateful to her family—Glen, Karl, and Angela—for their patience, understanding, encouragement, and humor throughout.

Unit One
An Approach to Academic Writing

Graduate students face a variety of writing tasks as they work toward their chosen degrees. Naturally, these tasks will vary from one degree program to another. They are, however, similar in two respects. First, the tasks become progressively more complex and demanding the farther you go in the program. Second (with few exceptions), they need to be written "academically." In the first six units of this textbook, we focus on the writing tasks that may be required in the earlier stages of a graduate career. In the last two units we look a little farther ahead.

We begin by providing an overview of some important characteristics of academic writing. Academic writing is a product of many considerations: audience, purpose, organization, style, flow, and presentation (fig. 1).

Audience

Even before you write, you need to consider your audience. The audience for most graduate students will be an instructor, who is presumably quite knowledgeable about the assigned writing topic. To be successful in your writing task, you need to have an understanding of your audience's expectations and prior knowledge, because these will affect the content of your writing.

Task One

Consider the following statements. For whom were they written? What are the differences between the two?

1a. Thermal systems is a very broad field involving many separate fields of engineering.
1b. Thermal systems is an interdisciplinary field which involves the traditional disciplines of thermodynamics, heat transfer, fluid mechanics, mass transfer, and chemical kinetics.

AUDIENCE

PURPOSE

ORGANIZATION

STYLE

FLOW

PRESENTATION

Fig. 1. Considerations in academic writing

Now consider the following. For whom were these written? What are the differences between the two?

2a. A consonant is a speech sound produced by either closing or constricting the vocal tract.

2b. A speech sound produced by either closing or constricting the vocal tract is called a consonant.

Task Two

Now write a one-sentence definition of a term in your field for two different audiences: one will be graduate students in a totally unrelated field, while the other consists of fellow students in your own graduate program. Exchange your definition with a partner and discuss how your definitions differ.

Purpose and Strategy

Audience, purpose, and strategy are typically interconnected. If the audience knows less than the writer, the writer's purpose is often instructional (as in a textbook). If the audience knows more than the writer, the writer's purpose is usually to *display* familiarity, expertise, and intelligence. The latter is a common situation for the graduate student writer.

The interesting question now arises as to what strategy a graduate student can use to make a successful *display*. Consider the case of an Asian student who in the United States calls himself "Gene." Gene is enrolled in a master's program in public health. He has nearly finished his first writing assignment, which focuses on one aspect of health care costs in the United States This is a short assignment rather than a major research paper. The deadline is approaching and there is no more time for further data analysis. He wants to make a good impression with his concluding paragraph. He believes (rightly) that final impressions are important.

Gene (quite appropriately) begins his last paragraph by reminding his audience (i.e., his instructor) of what he has done in the paper. He begins as follows:

Conclusion

The aim of this paper has been to examine the health care costs of non-profit and for profit hospitals in the United States. In particular I have examined the effects of decreasing co-payments under each system.

So far, so good. His first attempt at completing his paper is as follows:

As the tables show, in non-profit hospitals, costs increased by 4.8%, while in for-profit hospitals, increases averaged 24.7%. As I have explained, the probable cause of this difference is that physicians in for-profit hospitals ordered many more tests when the co-payment was reduced.

What do you think of this?

Gene does not like the conclusion. "Wrong strategy," he says. "This is just repeating what I have already written; it makes it seem that I have run out of ideas. There is nothing new here; my paper dies at the end."

Gene tries again. "This time," he says to himself, "I will take my results, summarize them, and then try to connect them to some wider issue. That's a better strategy." Here is his second version:

As the tables show, in non-profit hospitals the effect was relatively minor, whereas in for-profit contexts cost increases were considerable. In the latter case, the reduced co-payments apparently gave rise to a noticeable increase in the number of tests ordered by physicians. These findings support other studies which show that cost containment may prove very difficult in a "free market" medical economy.

Gene likes this version; however, he is also worried. He knows—but he has not said so anywhere yet—that there is a serious problem with the data he has been using. The comparison between the two types of hospitals may not be valid.

He now writes:

The findings should be considered somewhat provisional at this stage. This is because the patients in the two systems have not been equated for such variables as patient income, age, and level of satisfaction with the health-care provider.

Gene is asking himself the question: Is it better to admit that there are problems with the data, or not to mention this at all? Which strategy is better? Will I appear more or less intelligent by discussing the problem? And if I do discuss it, should I put it right at the end?

Task Three

What advice would you give Gene? Write down your suggestions in note form. Then edit or rewrite his final paragraph to reflect your advice.

Organization

Information is presented to readers in a structured format. Even short pieces of writing have regular, predictable patterns of organization. You can take advantage of these patterns, so that readers can still follow, even if you make errors.

A clear, predictable pattern of organization can be seen in the following letters. The first is a good-news letter.

Dear Ms. Wong:

Thank you for your interest in our   ACKNOWLEDGMENT
university. On behalf of the Dean of
the Graduate School, I congratulate
you on being accepted to the pro-   GOOD NEWS
gram in Aerospace Engineering to
begin study at the master level. This
letter is your official authorization to
register for Fall 1994. As a reflection
of the importance the Graduate
School places on the ability of its
students to communicate effectively,
the Graduate School requires all
new students whose native language   ADMINISTRATIVE
is not English to have their En-   DETAILS
glish evaluated. Specific details for
this procedure are given in the en-
closed information packet.

We look forward to welcoming you   WELCOMING
to Midwestern University and wish   CLOSE
you success in your academic career.

Sincerely,

Task Four

Now here is the bad-news letter. After you read it, place the labels
for the four parts in the correct spaces.

preparation for bad news   bad news   close   acknowledgment

Dear Mr. Lee:

Thank you for your interest in   _____
the graduate program in In-
dustrial and Operations Engineering. We have now finished

our rigorous review process
for Fall 1994 applications. We
received an unusually high
number of applications for the
Fall term and we unfor-
tunately had to limit the number we could accept. While
your background is impres-
sive, I regret to inform you
that your application to the
program has not been ac-
cepted. Given your excellent
qualifications, I trust you will
be able to pursue your academic interests elsewhere and
wish you luck in your
further endeavors.

Sincerely,

The acceptance letter is organized differently than the rejection letter. The news in the letter does not come at the same place. Why do
you suppose this is?

The writer of the good-news letter wants the correspondence to
continue, while the writer of the bad-news letter wants the correspondence to end. Can you think of any other difference in purpose?

Academic writing also employs a variety of organizational patterns. You are already familiar with external organization features,
such as chapters, sections, and paragraphs. You should become familiar with internal organization as well. One very common strategy in academic writing is to organize information in terms of
problem-solution (Hoey 1983). This pattern usually has four parts:

1. Description of a situation
2. Identification of a problem
3. Description of a solution
4. Evaluation of the solution

Task Five

Draw boxes around and label the four parts of this problem-solution text. The first part has been done for you.

1. Description of a situation

International students often study English for many years before going to an English-speaking country to pursue a graduate degree. Their study of English usually focuses on grammar and reading, with little attention paid to speaking, writing, and listening (Belcher 1994). Despite their many years of English instruction, after arriving in an English-speaking country, many international students understandably find that their interactive skills are weak. In particular, they often experience difficulty actually using their English, which can result in frustration and misunderstanding. Recent research has shown that one way to overcome this frustration is to arrange a language exchange with a native speaker of English who wants to learn a foreign language (Brennan 1991). In this arrangement, the two partners exchange their knowledge of their native languages, thus providing a comfortable learning environment. Language exchanges can be one of the best ways to enhance one's language skills, because they are done on a one-to-one basis.

Now discuss with a partner the following two questions. How serious is the problem? How would you evaluate the solution?

Task Six

Here is another passage with the same structure. Read it and answer the questions that follow. Sentence numbers have been added here (and in subsequent texts) for ease of reference.

[1]Madagascar has one of the world's oldest systems of natural reserves. [2]This system, established during the early 1900s, was designed to protect lemurs and other animal species unique to the island. [3]However, due to severe economic hardship, this island country lacks the funds to properly manage the reserves; as a result, many species risk extinction. [4]One recent solution to this problem has been offered by the international community. [5]If Madagascar begins to better protect its reserves, its foreign debt will be reduced. [6]This incentive should lead to some level of improvement.

(Based on information from *Scientific American*, January 1993)

1. For what type of audience was this written?

2. What assumptions does the author make about the audience's knowledge background?

3. What is the author's purpose?

4. What does *this problem* in sentence 4 refer to?

5. What does *this incentive* in sentence 6 refer to?

6. What does the author think of the solution?

7. If the writer had thought that the solution would not work, what might he have written for the last sentence? In such a case, would this last sentence be enough to complete the text? If not, what would need to be added?

Style

Academic writers need to be sure that their communications are written in the appropriate style. The style of a particular piece must not only be consistent, but must also be proper for the message being conveyed and for the audience. A formal research report written in informal English may be considered too simplistic, even if the actual ideas and/or data are complex.

One difficulty in using the appropriate style is knowing what is considered academic and what is not. Academic style is not used in all academic settings. Lectures are generally delivered in a relatively nonacademic style. It is not uncommon to hear lecturers use words and phrases like *stuff*, *things*, *bunch*, or *a whole lot of*, which would not be appropriate for an academic writing task. They may also use elaborate metaphors and other vivid expressions to enliven their speaking style. While it is valuable to understand and acquire such language for personal use, it is not generally appropriate for academic writing. This *vocabulary shift* is indeed the most salient feature of academic writing.

Language Focus: The Vocabulary Shift

A distinctive feature of academic writing style is choosing the more formal alternative when selecting a verb, noun, or other part of speech.

Verbs

English often has two (or more) choices to express an action or occurrence. The choice is often between a phrasal or prepositional verb (verb + preposition) and a single verb, the latter with Latinate origins. Often in lectures and other instances of everyday spoken English, the verb + preposition is used; however, for written academic style, the preferred choice is a single verb wherever possible. This is one of the most dramatic stylistic shifts from informal to formal style.

Researchers *looked at* the way strain *builds up* around a fault.
(less formal style)

Researchers *observed* the way strain *accumulates* around a fault. (academic style)

Task Seven

Choose a verb from the list that reduces the informality of each sentence. Note that you may need to add tense to the verb from the list.

| assist | reduce | create | investigate | raise |
| establish | increase | determine | fluctuate | eliminate |

1. Expert Systems can *help out* the user in the diagnosis of problems. _____

2. This program was *set up* to improve access to medical care.

   _____

3. Research expenditures have *gone up* to nearly $350 million.

   _____

4. The use of optical character readers (OCRs) should *cut down* the number of problems with the U.S. mail service.

   _____

5. Researchers have *found out* that this drug has serious side effects. _____

6. Building a nuclear power plant will not *get rid of* the energy problem completely. _____

7. Researchers have been *looking into* this problem for 15 years now. _____

8. This issue was *brought up* during the investigation.

   _____

9. Engineers can *come up with* better designs using CAD.

   _____

10. The emission levels have been *going up and down.*

    _____

Task Eight

Reduce the informality of each sentence by substituting a single verb for the one in italics.

1. The implementation of computer-integrated-manufacturing (CIM) has *brought about* some serious problems.

   _____

2. The process should be *done over* until the desired results are achieved. _____

3. Plans are being made to *come up with* a database containing detailed environmental information for the region.

   _____

4. Subtle changes in the earth's crust were *picked up* by these new devices. _____

5. Proposals to construct new nuclear reactors have *met with* great resistance from environmentalists. _____

   _____

Nouns and Other Parts of Speech

English has a very rich vocabulary derived from many languages. Because of this, there may be more than one way to express an idea. You should strive to choose words that are less informal in nature and also precise. In lectures, you will likely hear less formal speech; however, in writing you should use a more formal form if one exists.

Task Nine

Which of the underlined words would be more suitable for an academic paper?

1. The government has made *good* / *considerable* progress in solving environmental problems.
2. We *got* / *obtained* encouraging results.
3. The results of *a lot of* / *numerous* different projects have been *pretty good* / *encouraging*.
4. A loss of jobs is one of *the things that will happen* / *consequences* if the process is automated.

Supply a more academic word or phrase for the one underlined in each sentence.

5. The reaction of the officials was *sort of* negative. _____

6. The economic outlook is *mighty nice*. _____

7. The future of Federal funding is *up in the air*. _____

8. America's major automakers are planning to *get together* on the research needed for more fuel efficient cars. _____

Language Focus: Formal Grammar and Style

The following are some nonvocabulary-related recommendations for maintaining a formal academic writing style.

1. Avoid contractions.

Export figures *won't* improve until the economy is stronger. →
Export figures *will not* improve until the economy is stronger.

2. Use the more appropriate formal negative forms.

not . . . any → no
not . . . much → little
not . . . many → few

The analysis *didn't* yield *any* new results. →
The analysis yielded *no* new results.

The government *didn't* allocate *much* funding for the program. →
The government allocated *little* funding for the program.

This problem *doesn't* have *many* viable solutions. →
This problem has *few* viable solutions.

3. Limit the use of "run on" expressions, such as "and so forth" *lazy*
and "etc." → *not specific*

These semiconductors can be used in robots, CD players, *etc.* →
These semiconductors can be used in robots, CD players, *and*
    other electronic devices.

4. Avoid addressing the reader as "you" (except, of course, if you are
writing a textbook).

You can see the results in Table 1. →
The results can be seen in Table 1.

5. Limit the use of direct questions.

What can be done to lower costs? →
We now need to consider what can be done to lower costs. *or*
We now need to consider how costs may be lowered.

6. Place adverbs within the verb.

Adverbs often are placed midposition rather than in the initial or
final positions. In informal English, adverbs often occur as clauses
at the beginning or end of sentences.

Then the solution can be discarded. →
The solution can *then* be discarded.

The blood is withdrawn *slowly*. →
The blood is *slowly* withdrawn.

In summary, in one way or another most of our recommendations are designed to help you maintain a scholarly and objective tone in your writing. This does not mean (and we have not said) that you should *never* use *I* or *we* in your writing. The use of *I* or *we* does not make a piece of writing informal. The vocabulary shift and some of the other features we have mentioned are more important for maintaining a consistent academic style. In fact, you may remember that Gene wrote, "I have examined . . ."

Task Ten

Reduce the informality of each sentence.

1. If you fail the exam, you can't enter the university.

2. OK, what are the causes of deformation? Many possibilities exist.

3. You can clearly see the difference between these two processes.

4. A small bit of ammonium dichromate is added to the gelatin solution gradually.

5. These special tax laws have been enacted in six states: Illinois, Iowa, Ohio, etc.

6. The subjects didn't have much difficulty with the task.

Task Eleven

Now that you have become more familiar with some of the conventions of academic writing, write a one-paragraph problem-solution text about a problem in your country. Refer, if you like, to the Madagascar text on page 14. Your audience is a group of American peers and professors interested in your country. Follow the style guidelines on pages 18–19 as you write.

Flow

Another important consideration for successful communication is flow—moving from one statement in a text to the next. Naturally, establishing a clear connection of ideas is important to help your reader follow the text.

Task Twelve

Consider the following passages. Underline the parts in passage *b* that differ from passage *a*. Why does *b* have better "flow" than *a?*

a. Lasers have found widespread application in medicine. Lasers play an important role in the treatment of eye disease and the prevention of blindness. The eye is ideally suited for laser surgery. Most of the eye tissue is transparent. The frequency and focus of the laser beam can be adjusted according to the absorption of the tissue. The beam "cuts" inside the eye with minimal damage to the surrounding tissue—even the tissue between the laser and the incision. Lasers are effective in treating some causes of blindness. Other treatments are not. The interaction between laser light and eye tissue is not fully understood.

b. Lasers have found widespread application in medicine. For example, they play an important role in the treatment of eye disease and the prevention of blindness. The eye is ideally suited for laser surgery because most of the eye tissue is transparent. Because of this transparency, the frequency and focus of the laser beam can be adjusted according to the absorption of the tissue so that the beam "cuts" inside the eye with minimal damage to the surrounding tissue—even the tissue between the laser and the incision. Lasers are also more effective than other methods in treating some causes of blindness. However, the interaction between laser light and eye tissue is not fully understood.

Language Focus: Linking Words and Phrases

Linking words and phrases can help a writer maintain flow and establish clear relationships between ideas. Table 1 lists some of the more common linking words and phrases, arranged according to their function and grammatical use. Sentence connectors raise a small, but important issue, namely punctuation. The flowchart in figure 2 can help you choose appropriate punctuation.

Then

TABLE 1. Linking Words and Phrases

	Subordinators	Sentence Connectors	Phrase Linkers
Addition		furthermore in addition moreover	in addition to
Adversative	although even though despite the fact that	however nevertheless	despite in spite of
Cause and Effect	because since	therefore as a result consequently hence thus*	because of due to as a result of
Clarification		in other words that is i.e.	
Contrast	while whereas	in contrast however on the other hand conversely	unlike
Illustration		for example for instance	
Intensification		on the contrary as a matter of fact in fact	

*Note that *thus* may also be used in nonfinite clauses of result. *The scandal deepened, thus causing the Minister to resign.*

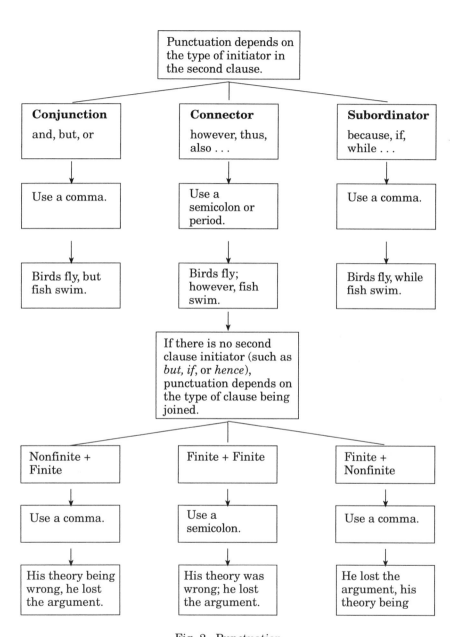

Fig. 2. Punctuation

Task Thirteen

Edit the following passage by adding semicolons or commas where necessary.

[1]Aluminum alloys are now more important in the automobile industry than ever before. [2]The government is pressuring the industry to produce cars of high quality and with high fuel efficiency hence car makers are replacing traditional iron-based alloys with aluminum alloys. [3]Aluminum alloy parts are typically one-third to one-half the weight of those made with steel as a result cars with all aluminum parts use approximately 50% less fuel than those with steel components. [4]Although most aluminum alloys are soft they can have a higher tensile strength than steel. [5]Adequate alloy and solution treatment can increase their tensile strength thus resulting in a vehicle with good impact capacity.

Task Fourteen

Supply linking words or phrases that enhance the flow of the passage. Look carefully at the punctuation to help you make an appropriate choice.

[1]Many modern artists are using computers in their work because these machines enable the artist to be more creative. [2]Some artists believe computers will gain in popularity; _____ _____, others feel they will have at best a fleeting presence in the art world. [3]The computer is not a conventional art tool exactly like a brush, pencil, or hammer; _____, it is a tool that provides greater flexibility. [4]_____

_____ the use of computers for artistic purposes seems somewhat unusual, researchers believe their use will indeed become more widespread in the next century. [5]Changes can be made quickly and easily when artists use computers. [6]_____, copying portions of a painting, drawing, or musical composition can be done with a keystroke, _____ saving the artist considerable time. [7]_____ some initial resistance, the artistic community is beginning to realize that technology can indeed play a role in creativity.

Language Focus: *this* + Summary Word

Another way to maintain flow is to use *this/these* + a noun to join ideas together. Consider the following sentences.

> ESL lecturers know that students need to understand the differences between formal and informal language. However, *this understanding* cannot usually be acquired quickly.

What does *this understanding* refer to?

Consider the following sentences.

> In recent years, the number of students applying to Ph.D. programs has increased steadily, while the number of places available has remained constant. *This situation* has resulted in intense competition for admission.

What does *this situation* refer to? What is the effect of using *this* instead of *that*?

The phrases in italics contain a summary noun or word that refers back to the idea in the previous sentence. These phrases *summarize* what has already been said.

Task Fifteen

Complete the following.

1. According to a recent survey, 26% of all American adults, down from 38% thirty years ago, now smoke. This _____ can be partly attributed to the mounting evidence linking smoking and fatal diseases, such as cancer.

   a. decline b. reduction c. improvement d. decrease e. drop

   Can you think of any other nouns that could complete the sentence?

2. Early in September each year, the population of Ann Arbor, Michigan, suddenly increases by about 20,000 as students arrive for the new academic year. This _____ changes the character of the town in a number of ways.

   a. influx   b. increase   c. invasion   d. rise   e. jump

   Can you think of any other nouns that could complete the sentence?

3. Nowadays, laptop computers are lighter, more powerful, and easier to use than they were five years ago. These _____ have led to an increase in the sales of these machines.

   a. changes   b. developments   c. advances   d. improvements

Look back at the Madagascar text on p. 14. Can you identify the summary words?

Task Sixteen

Choose a summary word from the list to complete each sentence.

number	improvement	trend	fall	support	increase
amount	assurance	risk	drop	proposals	measures

1. In the United States, the levels of lead, carbon monoxide, and sulfur dioxide have fallen between 1978 and 1987. Despite this _____, the air is still contaminated by many carcinogens.

2. Ozone levels in the United States increased 5% from 1986–87, another 15% from 1987–88, and an additional 10% from 1988–90. Environmental Protection Agency (EPA) officials are concerned that if this _____ continues, serious environmental damage may occur.

3. The EPA has revealed that 20 of the 320 known toxic chemicals in the air probably cause more than 2,000 cases of cancer annually. While this _____ may not seem high, it is still a cause for concern.

4. The EPA states that individuals living near chemical plants have a higher than normal chance of developing cancer. This _____ has been substantiated by numerous studies.

5. The Chemical Manufacturers Association has decided it will more strongly support the pollution control efforts of the EPA. This _____ was a major factor in the drafting of new regulations.

6. Lawmakers in southern California are proposing banning the sale of new charcoal grills, requiring sophisticated pollution control devices, and demanding that by the next century 40% of all cars and buses run on clean fuel, such as methanol. These _____ may indeed become law in the near future.

Task Seventeen

Provide summary words to improve the flow of the passage.

[1]A 1986 study of 7,000 recovering alcoholics showed that 3% were under age 20 and 18% were between 21 and 30. [2]Moreover, the study revealed that the average age of alcoholics seems to be falling. [3]This _____ worries health officials. [4]In the past, alcohol addiction was considered a social problem closely related to criminal or immoral behavior. [5]However, today this _____ is no longer widely held. [6]Many alcoholics have lived through difficult childhoods, divorces, and professional disappointment. [7]Even so, these _____ are not good predictors of who will become an alcoholic. [8]In a recent study, children of alcoholics were found to be four times as likely as children of nonalcoholics to be alcoholics—even when raised by nonalcoholic parents. [9]This _____ has led researchers to believe there is a genetic link in alcoholism.

Presentation

Most instructors tolerate small errors in language in papers written by nonnative speakers—for example, mistakes in article or preposition usage. However, errors that could have been avoided by careful proofreading are generally considered less acceptable. These include the use of an incorrect homophone (a word that sounds exactly like another such as *too/to/two*); basic grammar errors (e.g., in subject-verb agreement); and misspelled words, including those that are not identified in a computer spell-check routine.

In addition, your presented work is more likely to receive a positive response if you perform the following tasks.

1. Consider the overall format of your written work.

   Does your paper look as if it has been carefully prepared?
   Are there clear paragraphs?
   Is the line spacing appropriate?

2. Proofread for careless grammar mistakes.

   Do subjects and verbs agree?
   Have the appropriate verb tenses been used?
   Have the articles *a*, *an*, and *the* been used when necessary?
   Is *the* used too much?

3. Check for misspelled words, even if you have spell-checked your work.

   Has the correct homophone been used?
   Did the spell-check routine miss anything?

Task Eighteen

What type of visual impression would the page in figure 3 give a reader? What advice would you give the student who turned in this paper?

Fig.3

Task Nineteen

The paragraph division is fine for this next passage, but there are numerous small mistakes in grammar. Can you identify and correct them? (Because some of the errors are in article usage, you might wish to refer to Appendix One.)

The discovery of fossil fuels have had a big effect on development of cities. The use of the automobile has become most important element supporting the modern society. And, since a few decade ago, the finiteness of natural resources is a source of heated controversy. The cities and its development will certainly be affected.
  Greater focus on accessible public transportations is one change in current urban planning discussions. It widely believes that there will be an effort to redesign cities in order promote the use of public transportation. . . .

Task Twenty

The following short passage has been spell-checked. Although all the words are spelled correctly as far as the spell-check program is concerned, seven usage and spelling errors remain. Can you identify and correct them?

Their is considerable doubt weather this solution will be affective.

The initial reaction too the report has not been complementary.

In fact many observers belief that collapse of the system is eminent.

Now try correcting this poem.

I have a spelling checker,   I've run this poem threw it,

It came with my PC.   I'm sure your please to no,

It plainly marks four my revue   It's letter perfect in it's weigh,

Mistakes I cannot sea.   My checker tolled me sew.

(Source unknown)

Positioning

Now that you are familiar with the most important characteristics of academic writing, you are ready to "position" or establish yourself as a junior member of your chosen field (see fig. 4).

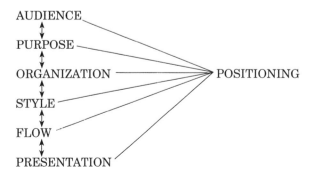

Fig. 4. Positioning

Task Twenty-one

Mark these writing characteristics as *H* (helpful for positioning) or *U* (unhelpful for positioning). In some cases there is room for disagreement.

1. Choosing any writing style that you like   _____
2. Expressing enthusiasm and commitment   _____
3. Writing in a formal academic style   _____
4. Making broad generalizations   _____
5. Being cautious about generalizations   _____
6. Using references   _____
7. Writing only from experience and personal knowledge   _____
8. Reevaluating the work of authorities in the field   _____

Can you explain your choices?

Unit Two
Writing General-Specific Texts

Each remaining unit in this book deals with a particular kind of writing task. We have chosen to begin with a type of text sometimes called general-specific (GS) because its structure involves general-to-specific movement. There are three reasons to begin with GS texts. They are quite common in graduate student writing, they are comparatively simple, and they are often used as introductions for longer pieces of writing. You may need to produce a GS text for

a. an answer to an examination question,
b. an opening paragraph of an assignment,* or
c. a background (or scene-setting) paragraph to an analysis or discussion.*

GS texts usually begin with *one* of the following:

a. a short or extended definition,
b. a contrastive or comparative definition, or
c. a generalization or purpose statement.

As their name implies, GS texts move from broad statements to narrower ones. However, they often widen out again in the final sentence. The shape is similar to that of a glass or cup (see fig. 5). *cf.13)*

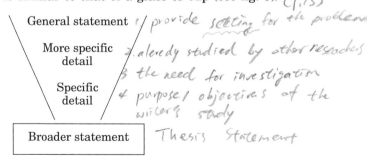

General statement / *provide setting for the problem*

More specific detail / *already studied by other researchers*

3 the need for investigation

Specific detail / *4 purpose / objectives of the writers study*

Broader statement | *Thesis Statement*

Fig. 5. Shape of GS texts   *p18. C9*

*Both *b* and *c* may also take the form of a descriptive summary (see Unit Five).

5. optional statement
give a value justification
for carrying at the study

Task One

Here is a short example of a GS text. Read the text and answer the questions that follow. Sentence numbers have been added here (and in subsequent texts) for ease of reference.

Writing

[1]Writing is a complex sociocognitive process involving the construction of recorded messages on paper or on some other material, and, more recently, on a computer screen. [2]The skills needed to write range from making the appropriate graphic marks, through utilizing the resources of the chosen language, to anticipating the reactions of the intended readers. [3]The first skill area involves acquiring a writing system, which may be alphabetic (as in European languages) or nonalphabetic (as in many Asian languages). [4]The second skill area requires selecting the appropriate grammar and vocabulary to form acceptable sentences and then arranging them in paragraphs. [5]Third, writing involves thinking about the purpose of the text to be composed and about its possible effects on the intended readership. [6]One important aspect of this last feature is the choice of a suitable style. [7]Because of these characteristics, writing is not an innate natural ability like speaking but has to be acquired through years of training or schooling.

1. The "shape" of this passage is something like this. Complete the diagram.

   1) _____

     2) <u>Main skills involved</u>_____

       3) <u>Skill area 1</u>____

       4) _____

       5) <u>Skill area 3</u>____

         6) _____

     7) <u>Learning to write</u>_____

2. The author of this passage has decided it is too short. Here are three additional statements. Where would you place them?

   a. Although writing systems have been in existence for about 5,000 years, even today only a minority of the world's population knows how to write.

   b. Mandarin, for example, uses an ideograph system that is particularly difficult to learn.

   c. Because of its complexity, the study of writing has become a multidisciplinary activity.

The GS *Writing* passage could have been a short answer to an in-class exam, perhaps in English education or psychology. The exam question could have been:

Outline briefly the main characteristics of two of the following. Write seven to ten sentences.

   1. Writing
   2. Nonverbal communication
   3. Speech

Alternatively, the passage on writing could also have been the *opening* paragraph to a longer assignment—perhaps one asking the student to analyze some experimental data or to assess the current state of research.

As in many GS texts, the "Writing" passage began with a definition. Definitions are a common way of getting started; they are "hooks" from which GS paragraphs can be hung. Such paragraphs typically open with full-sentence definitions. Textbooks, in contrast, often introduce the definitional information as a minor part of the sentence, as in the following example.

The majority of corporate profits, or *earnings after all the operating expenses have been deducted*, are subject to tax by the government.

Textbook definitional information is used to clarify terms that may be unfamiliar to the reader. However, this is not your task, since your audience is already familiar with the terms and expects you to write a text that *demonstrates* your understanding of complex concepts.

In the next part of this unit, we will highlight certain aspects of the structure of these key definitional sentences. Then we will consider more extended definitions, contrastive definitions (e.g., organic versus inorganic chemistry), and comparative definitions (i.e., discussions of the advantages and disadvantages of competing definitions).

Sentence Definitions

Let us start by looking at sentence definitions. A sentence definition is often a useful starting point for a GS paragraph. In a formal sentence definition, such as the examples that follow, the term being defined is first assigned to a class or group to which it belongs and then distinguished from other terms in the class.

A sole proprietorship is a business which is owned and operated by one individual for personal profit.

To what class does the sole proprietorship belong? How is it different from other members of the class? How would you define a partnership?

A star is a celestial body that shines by itself and whose source of energy is nuclear fusion occurring in its core.

To what class does a star belong? Can you think of other celestial bodies? How is a star different from these?

Annealing is a metalworking process in which a material is subjected to elevated temperatures for a period of time to cause structural or electrical changes in its properties.

To what class does annealing belong? How is it different from other members of the class, such as hammering or welding?

Notice that each of these definitions is completed by some form of restrictive clause and has the structure shown here.

	term		class		specific detail
(A)	_____	is (a)	_____	*wh*-word*	_____ .
				that	
A	solar cell	is a	device	which	converts the energy of sunlight into electric energy.

Language Focus: The Grammar of Definitions

Notice the use of the indefinite articles *a* and *an* in the first part of the definitions. (For a more complete discussion of articles, see Appendix One.)

A sole proprietorship is a business . . .
Annealing is a metalworking process . . .
A star is a celestial body . . .
Writing is a sociocognitive process . . .

In most definitions, the indefinite article is used before both the term and the class. The indefinite article before the class indicates that you are classifying a term, as you do in a definition. The indefinite article before the term conveys the meaning that any representative of this term will fit the assigned class. This use of the indefinite article or the absence of an initial article signals a definition. (As you know, *a* is used for countable nouns, but no article is used before uncountable nouns.)

You may ask why *the* is not used in a formal sentence definition. Take a look at the following sentences.

a. A disinfectant is *an* agent capable of destroying disease-causing microorganisms.
b. A disinfectant is *the* agent capable of destroying disease-causing micro-organisms.

---

*Although the *Chicago Manual of Style* and other style manuals recommend using *that* instead of *which* in restrictive relative clauses, research shows that *which* continues to be used in definition statements. Therefore, we have used both *which* and *that* in the sample definitions presented in this unit.

Sentence *a* classifies the term; it does not refer to a particular representative. Sentence *b*, however, identifies or describes the term. Further, in *b*, it is implied that there has been some previous mention of other agents that are not capable of destroying disease-causing microorganisms.*

Task Two

Insert the article *a* or *an* where necessary in the following definitions.

1. Helium is gas which consists of two protons, two neutrons, and two electrons.

2. Labor union is organization of workers formed to improve their economic status and working conditions.

3. White dwarf is star that is unusually faint given its extreme temperature.

4. Rice is cereal grain that usually requires subtropical climate and abundance of moisture for growth.

5. Transduction is technique in which genes are inserted into host cell by means of viral infection.

6. Heat is form of energy which can be transmitted through solid and liquid media by conduction.

Now let us turn to the grammar of the second part of a sentence definition. The distinguishing information in the restrictive relative clause can be introduced by either a full or a reduced relative clause. There are two common ways of reducing a restrictive relative. One involves a simple deletion, while the other involves a change in word form or an entire word. Although there have been claims that reduced relatives are uncommon in academic English, this is not the

---

*There is one main exception to the absence of *the* in formal definitions; this occurs in *explanations* of fields, as in "Phonetics is *the* study of speech sounds."

case. Reduced relatives are often preferred because they are shorter and "snappier."

Deletions

You may reduce the restrictive relative if

1. the relative clause consists only of the relative pronoun, the verb *to be*, and one or more prepositional phrases;

    A gill is an external respiratory organ *which is* in the gill chamber at the rear of the mouth of most aquatic animals. →
    A gill is an external respiratory organ in the gill chamber at the rear of the mouth of most aquatic animals.

    Enamel, in dentistry, is a hard, white inorganic material *that is* on the crown of a tooth. →
    Enamel, in dentistry, is a hard, white inorganic material on the crown of a tooth.

2. the relative clause consists of a passive verb plus some *additional* information;

    A theater is a building *which has been* specifically designed for dramatic performances. →
    A theater is a building specifically designed for dramatic performances.

    A collagen is a white, inelastic protein *that is* formed and maintained by fibroblasts. →
    A collagen is a white, inelastic protein formed and maintained by fibroblasts.

3. the relative clause contains the relative pronoun, an adjective ending in *-ble*, plus *additional* information.

    A robot is a multiprogrammable device *which is* capable of performing the work of a human.
    A robot is a multiprogrammable device capable of performing the work of a human.

Change in Word or Word Form

You may reduce the relative clause if

1. the relative clause contains the verb *have*. In this case the relative pronoun and *have* can both be dropped and replaced by *with*;

> A parliament is a national governing body *which has* the highest level of legislative power within a state. →
> A parliament is a national governing body *with* the highest level of legislative power within a state.

2. the relative clause contains an active state verb (a verb that expresses a state or something that is going on). The relative pronoun is dropped and the verb changed to the *-ing* form. Exceptions to this are *to be* and *have*.

> Pollution is a form of contamination *that often* results from human activity. →
> Pollution is a form of contamination often *resulting* from human activity.

> A moon is a natural satellite *which orbits* around a planet. →
> A moon is a natural satellite *orbiting* around a planet.

> A depression is a serious economic downturn *that* originates from a variety of factors, including overexpansion of commerce, industry, or agriculture, bank failures, or war. →.
> A depression is a serious economic downturn *originating* from a variety of factors, including overexpansion of commerce, industry, or agriculture, bank failures, or war.

It is also important to note that a relative clause containing a modal auxiliary cannot be reduced.

Task Three

Edit the following by reducing the relative clauses *where possible*.

1. Aluminum is a lightweight metal that is often used for high-tension power transmission.

2. Heat is a form of energy which can be transmitted through solid and liquid media by conduction.

3. A brake is a device that is capable of slowing the motion of a mechanism.

4. A dome is generally a hemispherical roof which is on top of a circular, square, or other-shaped space.

5. Snow is a form of precipitation which results from the sublimation of water vapor into solid crystals at temperatures below 0°C.

6. An antigen is a substance which causes the formation of antibodies, the body's natural response to foreign substances.

7. A piccolo is a small flute that is pitched an octave higher than a standard flute.

8. An oocyte is a cell which undergoes meiosis to produce an ovum or egg.

9. A catalyst is a substance that can speed up the rate of a chemical reaction without changing its own structure.

10. A black hole is a celestial body which has approximately the same mass as the sun and a gravitational radius of about 3 km.

Now notice also that in a full relative clause, the relative pronoun can be preceded by a preposition. The relative pronoun *which* must be used in this type of restrictive relative clause. This construction is common in formal academic writing. These clauses cannot be reduced.

A foundation is a base *on* which a structure can be built.

Task Four

Complete the following definitions by inserting an appropriate preposition.

1. A thermometer is an instrument _____ which temperature can be measured.

2. Photosynthesis is a process _____ which sunlight is used to manufacture carbohydrates from water and carbon dioxide.

3. A credit bureau is an organization _____ which businesses can apply for financial information on potential customers.

4. An anhydride is a compound _____ which the elements of water have been removed.

5. An eclipse is a celestial event _____ which one body, such as a star, is covered by another, such as a planet.

6. An axis is an imaginary line _____ which a body is said to rotate.

Whereby is commonly used in formal writing instead of *by which, by means of which,* and *through which*.

Collective bargaining is a process *whereby* employers agree to discuss work-related issues with employee representatives.

In this section we make a few final comments on how information should be presented in a one-sentence definition. First, care should be taken to find the precise word or phrase for the class:

A microscope is an object . . . ,   is less precise than
A microscope is an *instrument* . . .

A vowel is a sound . . . ,   is less precise than
A vowel is a *speech sound* . . .

Task Five

Choose a word or phrase that assigns the following terms or phrases to a precise class. Use your dictionary, if necessary.

	Class
1. a consonant	_____
2. an ellipse	_____
3. an amplifier	_____
4. neon	_____
5. a parasite	_____
6. an electric motor	_____
7. lysine	_____
8. mitosis	_____
9. oxidation	_____
10. a myth	_____
11. (one of your own)	_____
12. (another of your own)	_____

Now consider the sentence definitions in set *a*.

a.1. A solar cell is a device that converts the energy of sunlight into electric energy.
  2. A foundation is a base on which a structure can be built.

and their less academic counterparts in set *b*.

b.1. A solar cell is something that changes sunlight into electricity.
  2. A foundation is a base a structure can be built *on*.

The sentences in set *b* are perfectly acceptable in spoken English or E-mail. However, they would not be the most effective means of establishing yourself in your academic field. In *b.1*, for instance, *something* is both too broad and informal, and the verb consists of a verb + preposition combination (mentioned in Unit One as something generally to be avoided in academic writing). In *b.2*, the placement of the preposition at the end of the sentence may be considered "wrong" by those who believe that an academic English sentence should never end with a preposition. While it is valuable to understand and acquire such structures for personal use, for example, in E-mail messages, they should be avoided in academic writing (see Appendix Three).

Here are two final pieces of advice about writing formal definitions. Avoid using any form of your term in the definition. Using the term itself in the definition can result in a circular definition and is likely to be noted as such by your audience.

Erosion is a process during which the surface of the earth *erodes*. →
Erosion is a process during which the surface of the earth is degraded by the effects of the atmosphere, weather, and human activity.

Finally, avoid using *when* and *where* in definitions. These are less appropriate for a formal definition.

Pollution is when the environment becomes contaminated as a result of human activity. →

Pollution is a form of environmental contamination resulting from human activity.

A fault is where there is a fracture in the earth's crust and the rock on one side of the fracture moves in relation to the rock on the other side. →
A fault is a fracture in the earth's crust in which the rock on one side of the fracture moves in relation to the rock on the other side.

Task Six

Now write a one-sentence definition for two of the following terms and for at least one term from your own field. Make sure you provide enough specific detail to distinguish your term from other members in its class.

a dormitory	a computer virus	a carcinogen
a bridge	a conductor	a market
a plane		

Exchange and discuss your definitions with a partner.

Extended Definitions

So far we have only dealt with sentence definitions. In some cases, one sentence may be enough before continuing with your GS passage (as with the text on writing at the beginning of this unit). However, in others, it may be relevant and important to expand your definition. In this way you can demonstrate your knowledge of a concept more fully. An extended definition usually begins with a *general*, one-sentence definition and then becomes more *specific* as additional details are provided. There may be a need to display one or more of the following.

An analysis of components (if you are defining an object)

A microscope is an optical instrument with which the apparent size of an object can be enhanced. A simple microscope consists of a double convex lens and a magnifying glass. A compound microscope, on the other hand, will contain more than one of each of these lenses, which are situated at the ends of a cylinder.

Examples

Pollution is a form of environmental contamination resulting from human activity. Some common forms of pollution are wastes from the burning of fossil fuels and sewage running into rivers. Even litter and excessive noise can be considered forms of pollution because of the impact they can have on the environment.

A sense of historical change and development

Perspective is a technique in art that is used to represent three-dimensional objects and depth relationships on a flat surface. Modern linear perspective (which involves making objects seem smaller the more distant they are from the observer) was probably first used in the 1400s by the artist Masaccio and the architects Filippo Brunelleschi and Leon Battista Alberti in Florence, Italy. Before this time, artists paid little attention to realistic perspective. In recent decades, many modern artists have returned to the practices of early artists and have abandoned realistic perspective.

A knowledge of applications

An acrylic plastic is a polymer which can take a high polish, is clear and transparent, and can be shaped while hot. Because of these and other characteristics, acrylic plastic is used in situations where glass is not suitable or desirable, for instance, in certain types of windshields.

An extended definition may also include information regarding operating principles or causes and effects. A description of operating principles is also known as a process analysis. A process analysis has some unique characteristics, which will be discussed in greater detail in Unit Three. Extended definitions may also include information about many other features, such as rarity and cost.

You can even go beyond the type of specific detail just described and display your breadth of understanding by discussing problems, exceptions, and future predictions.

An awareness of problems with or exceptions to the general definition.

Lateralization is a developmental process during which the two sides of the brain become specialized for different functions. As a child develops, the two sides of the brain become asymmetric in that each side controls different abilities. Language, for instance, is controlled by the left side of the brain, and certain types of pattern recognition by the right. However, there is some disagreement as to when this specialization is complete. Some researchers believe the process is not complete until puberty, while others maintain that the brain is lateralized by age five.

Future predictions

A compact disc (CD) is an optical storage medium onto which information has been recorded digitally. In a CD recording of sound, sound waves are converted into digital numbers and inscribed on the disc. The digital data on the disc is read by a laser beam, thus eliminating any form of mechanical friction that could distort sound quality. CDs can also be used to store images as well as information. As optical data storage techniques improve, CD technology will become more widespread and may someday entirely replace magnetic storage.

Notice in the above definition that the full name of the term *compact disc* is given before introducing and using the acronym (CD).

Task Seven

Now read the following extended definition and answer the questions that follow.

[1]Navigation is a process by which means of transport can be guided to their destination when the route has few or no landmarks. [2]Some of the earliest navigators were sailors, who steered their ships first by the stars, then with a compass, and later with more complicated instruments that measured the position of the sun. [3]We are reminded of this by the fact that the word *navigation* comes from the Latin word for "ship." [4]However, the history and importance of navigation changed radically in the 20th century with the development of aircraft and missiles, which fly in three dimensions. [5]Today, both ships and aircraft rely heavily on computerized navigational systems that can provide a continuous, immediate, and accurate report of position.

(Benny Bechor, student, minor editing)

1. What type of information is included in each of the sentences in the definition?

2. How is the passage organized?

3. What tenses are used for which sentences? Why?

4. Sentence 3 begins with *we*. Is this appropriate?

Notice how the paragraph moves from a very general statement at the beginning to specific details, then "widens out" again in the final sentence to describe the current status of navigation. This pattern is quite common in paragraphs of this type.

Task Eight

Here are the sentences of a GS passage on an unusual but interesting topic. Work with a partner to put them back in the correct order. Write *1* next to the first sentence, *2* next to the second, and so on.

Palindromes

___ a. The term itself comes from the ancient Greek word *palindromos* meaning "running back again."

___ b. Another good and more recent example is "If I had a Hi-Fi."

___ c. Some very common English words are palindromes, such as *pop*, *dad*, and *noon*.

___ d. A palindrome is a word or phrase that results in the same sequence of letters no matter whether it is read from left to right or from right to left.

___ e. One of the classic long palindromes is "A man, a plan, a canal, Panama."

___ f. Long palindromes are very hard to construct, and some word puzzlers spend immense amounts of time trying to produce good examples.

Task Nine

1. Write an extended definition of a term in your field of study as if you were taking an examination. You will have 10 to 15 minutes.
2. For homework, write an extended definition of another term in your field of study. Take as long as you like!

Contrastive Definitions

So far, we have concentrated on developing a text starting from the definition of a single term. Often, however, you may be asked to display your knowledge about two (or more) related terms. Consider, for example, the following pairs.

a. An optical and an electron microscope
b. Pollution and adulteration
c. Writing and copying
d. An acrylic and a polyester
e. Annealing and welding
f. A compact disc and magnetic tape
g. A good-news and bad-news letter
h. A star and a planet
i. Formal and informal English

If you were asked in an in-class examination to explain the differences between the members of each pair, how many could you do?

Read this *draft* of a contrastive definition.

[1]A patent, in law, is a document that grants an inventor sole rights to the production, use, or sale of an invention or process for a limited period of time. [2]The inventor is guaranteed the possibility to earn profit for a reasonable period, while the public is guaranteed eventual free use. [3]On the other hand, a copyright is a document that grants an originator of artistic work exclusive use of the artistic creation for a specific period of time. [4]Copyrights are issued to authors, playwrights, composers, artists, and publishers, who then have control over publication, sale, and production of their creations.

This is a good start, but the two terms have been presented rather independently. The passage does not reveal the writer's understanding that there is one major characteristic linking patents and copyrights, namely that they both have a legal basis. The writer has also not made clear the distinction between the two. One way to do this would be to say:

The former deals with ＿＿＿＿＿＿＿, while the latter is concerned with ＿＿＿＿＿＿.

Task Ten

How could you rewrite the passage using *the former* and *the latter*? The missing information could be placed either at the beginning or the end of the passage. Which strategy would result in the most effective presentation? Can you suggest other changes that might improve the passage?

Also note that the contrastive definitions naturally make use of contrastive connectors (see page 22).

Task Eleven

Write a contrastive definition using the information given in either table 2 or table 3, or write a contrastive definition for one of the pairs listed at the beginning of this section on page 49.

TABLE 2.   Speech Sounds

Vowels	Consonants
Common in all languages	Common in all languages
Produced by allowing unobstructed flow of air through the mouth	Produced by obstructing the flow of air through the mouth
No points of articulation or contact-position of tongue	Many points of articulation—lips, tongue and teeth, tongue and palate, etc.
Lip rounding important	Lip rounding rarely important
Voiced	Voiced or voiceless
Can easily be produced alone and can even constitute an entire word, e.g., *eye*	Many are difficult to produce without an accompanying vowel
Can carry pitch and loudness	Cannot carry pitch and loudness

TABLE 3.   Nuclear Reactions

Fission	Fusion
Releases energy stored in nucleus of an atom	Releases energy stored in nucleus of an atom
Occurs with heavy nuclei	Occurs with light nuclei
Neutrons bombard nuclei of atoms, splitting the nuclei apart	Energy released even greater than that released in fusion
Splitting releases energy	Two nuclei combine at high temperatures
Can occur in a nuclear reactor to generate electricity	One nuclei is formed along with a neutron, releasing energy
Could also occur spontaneously	Occurs in the sun and stars
Does not require extreme temperatures	Requires temperatures of 1,000,000°C
Fuel is usually uranium, which is expensive and difficult to extract	Fuel is hydrogen, an abundant element

Comparative Definitions

Comparative definitions are typically introductory sections of assignments. They can be used to display your knowledge of the complexities surrounding key terms in your field of study. There are basically two approaches to this type of task. One is to present a historical account of how a concept has changed over time. The other is to present an overview of how various experts today view a concept differently. Good comparative definitions often contain elements of each approach.

Task Twelve

Read the following comparative definition and answer the questions that follow. This passage is more complex than any we have presented so far. Use a dictionary to check the meaning of words you do not know.

Problems in Defining Humor

[1]Generally speaking, humor is a quality in an event or expression of ideas which often evokes a physical response of laughter in a person. [2]It is an evasive quality that over the centuries has been the subject of numerous theories attempting to describe its origins. [3]There are essentially three main theories of humor, each of which has a number of variants: the superiority theory, the incongruity theory, and the relief theory. [4]The superiority theory, which dates back to Aristotle, through Thomas Hobbes (1651) and Albert Rapp (1951), describes all humor as derisive. [5]In other words, people laugh at the misfortunes of others or themselves. [6]Humor is, therefore, a form of ridicule that involves the process of judging or degrading something or someone thought to be inferior.

[7]The incongruity theory, on the other hand, maintains that humor originates from disharmony or inappropriateness. [8]Koestler (1964), for example, argues that humor involves coexisting incompatible events. [9]In other words, when two opposite or opposing ideas or events exist at the same time, humor exists. [10]Finally, the relief theory rejects the notion that either superiority or in-

congruity are the bases for humor. [11]Rather, proponents of this theory believe that humor is a form of release from psychological tension. [12]Humor provides relief from anxiety, hostility, aggression, and sexual tension. [13]Humor gratifies repressed feelings that operate on an unconscious level. [14]Earlier psychologists, such as Freud, Dewey, and Kline, were strong proponents of this theory.

[15]More modern theories of humor are essentially variations of one of these three traditional ones. [16]For instance, Duncan (1985), in his superiority theory, states that humor is linked to social status. [17]Deckers and Buttram (1990) expand incongruity theory to include elements of schema theory.* [18]In their view, distinctions between and within schemata are necessary for an understanding of humor. [19]While each of these theories can explain some aspect of humor, none can successfully be applied to all instances of humor.

1. In which sentences are the competing theories introduced?

2. What verb tense is used to introduce the definitions of the various researchers? Why do you suppose this is?

3. Underline the sentence connectors in the passage. Why were they used?

4. What do you think might follow this discussion of humor theories? A presentation of the author's own definition of humor? An analysis of one event using the different theories? Something else?

5. Do you think the whole passage is a GS text, part of it is, or none of it is?

6. Does the passage mention a modern version of the relief theory?

---

*Schemata are the types of background knowledge that a person brings to a context. For instance, you may have schemata for going to a restaurant or for going to a birthday party.

7. Do you think that the author of this passage (Chris) has positioned herself as neutral, or do you think she has a preference? If you think she has a preference, what do you think it is? Why do you think so?

We will return to the writing of comparative summaries in Unit Five.

Generalizations

We have focused so far on starting GS passages with definitions. Of course, this is neither always necessary nor always appropriate. It is also possible to start with a factual generalization. Suppose, for instance, the topic assigned is "The English Language." Now, if we were to write on this topic as philologists, we might still open the text with a definition.

> English is a language that belongs to the West Germanic subgroup of the Indo-European language family. It began its history as a distinct tongue in England around 500 A.D.

However, in most other circumstances, it is more likely that we would start with a generalization.

a. In comparison to many of the world's better-known languages, English is relatively new. Indeed, the English of 600 years ago can be understood only by specialists.

b. Although Chinese has the greatest number of speakers, English is the most widely distributed language in the world today. This position derives from the fact that English is widely taught as a second language in schools and widely used in international communication.

Task Thirteen

Below you will find three pairs of sentences, each consisting of a definition and a generalization. When would it be better to begin a text with the first sentence in each pair rather than the second?

a.1. Russian is the first language of about 150 million inhabitants of the former Soviet Union.

2. Russian is a language belonging to the West Slavic subgroup of the Indo-European language family.

b.1. AIDS has emerged as a devastating infectious disease for which there is presently no cure.

2. AIDS is a disease caused by a virus that attacks the immune system.

c.1. A catalyst is a substance which increases the rate of a chemical reaction.

2. Catalyst technology has progressed quickly as researchers better understand the complex interactions of molecules.

Task Fourteen

Write a GS paragraph on your own first language or on a topic from your field of study. Begin with either a definition or a generalization.

Introduction

1. Description of a situation
2. I.D. of a problem
3. Description of a solution
4. Evalution of the solution

(Wld Ser p 78, 96)

Unit Three
Problem, Process, and Solution

In Unit Two, we explored one common kind of underlying structure to academic writing, that of general-to-specific movement. This structure will prove useful in later units, when producing data commentaries (Unit Four) or writing introductions to research papers (Unit Eight). In this unit, we explore and practice a second underlying structure in academic writing, that of problem-to-solution movement. This structure will again prove useful later on, when writing critiques (Unit Six) and once more in introductions. In addition, we have built into the problem-solution structure some discussion of process descriptions. In many cases, it makes sense to see describing the parts of a process as the *steps required* to provide a solution to some problem.

As we have seen, general-specific passages tend to be descriptive and expository. In contrast, problem-solution texts tend to be more argumentative and evaluative. In the former, then, graduate students will most likely position themselves as being informed and organized; in the latter as questioning and perceptive.

The Structure of Problem-Solution Texts

At the end of the last unit, we looked at some general statements about the English language. We begin this unit with a passage on a follow-up topic, organized as a problem-solution text.

Task One

The following passage is about the role of English today in research and scholarship. Before you read the passage, circle the answer of your choice to question 1. Briefly discuss your estimate with a partner.

1. What is the current percentage of research papers published in English—as opposed to other languages?

30%   40%   50%   60%   70%   80%   90%

Now read on.

The Role of English in Research and Scholarship

[1]There are many claims that a clear majority of the world's research papers are now published in English. [2]For example, in 1983 Eugene Garfield, President of the Institute for Scientific Information (ISI)[1], claimed that 80% of the world's scientific papers are written in English (Garfield 1983). [3]Comparable estimates have recently been produced for engineering, medicine, and nonclinical psychology.

[4]It is not clear, however, whether such high percentages for English provide an accurate picture of languages chosen for publication by researchers around the world. [5]The major difficulty is bias in the databases from which these high percentages are typically derived. [6]The databases are those established by the major abstracting and indexing services, such as the ISI indexes and Medline, which are predominantly located in the United States. [7]As a result, these services have tended to preselect papers that (*a*) are written in English and (*b*) originate in the northern hemisphere. [8]For these two reasons, it is probable that research in languages other than English is somewhat underrepresented.[2] [9]Indeed, Najjar (1988) showed that no Arabic language science journal was consistently covered by the Science Citation Index in the mid-1980s.

[10]We can hypothesize from the previous discussion that the role of English in research may be considerably inflated. [11]In fact, several small-scale studies bear this out: Throgmartin (1980) produced English percentages in the 40% range for

---

1. The Institute for Scientific Information (ISI) publishes the *Science Citation Index* (SCI), the *Social Science Citation Index* (SSCI), and the *Arts and Humanities Citation Index* (AHCI).

2. The ISI itself has concluded that it may underrepresent useful research from the lesser developing countries by a factor of two (Moravcsik 1985).

social sciences, and Velho and Krige (1984) showed a clear preference for publication in Portuguese among Brazilian agricultural researchers. [12]A complete bibliography on schistosomiasis, a tropical disease, by Warren and Newhill (1978) revealed an English language percentage of only 45%. [13]These studies would seem to indicate that a more accurate percentage for English would be around 50% rather than around 80%.

[14]However, so far no major international study exists to corroborate such a conclusion. [15]Until such a study is undertaken—perhaps by UNESCO—the true global picture of language use in research publication will remain open to doubt and disagreement. [16]Until such time, nonnative speakers of English will remain uncertain about how effective their publications are in their own languages.

2. The passage consists of four short paragraphs, which deal in turn with the four parts of the standard problem-solution text (see table 4). Are sentences 1, 4, 10, and 14 the key sentences in the passage? If not, which other sentences might you suggest? Would you suggest sentence 13, for example?

3. Where do you think the author (John) is more convinced? Is it in the statement of the problem in paragraph 2, or in the statement of the solution in paragraph 3? Why do you think this?

4. List (using name and year) the citations used by the author. Do you have any criticisms?

5. Do you have any evidence to contribute about the languages of publication in your own field? What about the languages of research publication in your home country?

TABLE 4. Parts of a Problem-Solution Text

Situation	Background information about claims for research English
Problem	Reasons for doubting the accuracy of the figures
Solution	Alternative data leading to more accurate figures
Evaluation	Assessment of the merits of the proposed answer

Language Focus: Midposition Adverbs

At the end of the section on style in Unit One (p. 19), we noted that adverbs tend to occur within the verb in formal academic writing. In this language focus, we develop this point a little further. First, look at some of these occurrences from sentences in the text in Task One.

1. ... are now published ...
3. ... have recently been produced ...
8. ... will be somewhat underrepresented ...

If *today* had been used in sentence 1, it would have occurred immediately after the verb:

> ... are published today in English.

In sentence 3 we have a three-part verb in the present perfect passive: *have been produced*. Notice that the adverb occurs after *have*.

Read through the text again and find the other four instances of midposition adverbs.

Problem Statements

Now let us turn our attention again to the Problem part of the text.

[4]It is not clear, however, whether such high percentages for English provide an accurate picture of languages chosen for publication by researchers around the world. [5]The major difficulty is bias in the databases from which these high percentages are typically derived. [6]The databases are those established by the major abstracting and indexing services, such as the ISI indexes and Medline, which are predominantly located in the United States. [7]As a result, these services have tended to preselect papers that (*a*) are written in English and (*b*) originate in the northern hemisphere. [8]For these two reasons, it is probable that research in languages other than English is somewhat underrepresented.[2] [9]Indeed, Najjar (1988) showed that no Arabic language science journal was consistently covered by the Science Citation Index in the mid-1980s.

1. In the opening words of the paragraph, it is not clear at this time that *however* is a signal that a problem will be introduced. The text then goes on to explain the problem in some detail. The author (John) wants to convince the reader that the problem is indeed a problem. How does he accomplish this?

2. Do you think *as a result* in sentence 7 follows naturally? Do you think it would improve the text to put footnote 2 in the main text?

3. How would you judge the amount of detail? Is it just right? Too much? Not enough? Would more mention of databases be helpful? Is a single example enough?

4. Can you give a case of possible bias in the data from your own field (or from your experience)?

5. How successful do you think the type of explanation employed in this text would be for other kinds of problems?

Procedures and Processes

The "Role of English" text is a typical *research question* example of a problem-solution text. In essence, it uses the problem-solution structure to *review* the current state of knowledge. The review approach allows the author to raise a question about the current state of knowledge and to offer a possible or part answer. However, the "classic" problem-solution texts are usually more *technical* in nature and may describe procedures and processes. We see this in the passage in Task Two.

Task Two

Read the following passage written by Chris and answer the questions that follow. The passage is a problem-solution text about an area in Chile that has a desert climate—the Atacama Desert.

Clouds and Fog as a Source of Water in Chile

[1]Many of Chile's poor, northern coastal villages have suffered in recent years from water shortages, despite the abundance of cloud cover and fog in the region. [2]When the cold air from the Pacific Ocean's Humboldt current mixes with the warm coastal air, a thick, wet fog, called *camanchaca* by the Andes Indians, forms along with clouds. [3]However, rather than developing into rain, the clouds and fog are quickly evaporated by the hot sun. [4]This absence of rainfall has imposed severe hardship on communities. [5]They cannot grow crops and must carefully ration their water, which has to be delivered by truck.

[6]One interesting solution to this problem is now being tested in the village of Chungungo, a village of 300. [7]Using conventional technology, researchers have redevised a centuries-old method to capture the water droplets of the fog. [8]In this method, triangular-weave polypropylene nets are attached to wooden support posts on El Tofo mountain to serve as water collectors. [9]Each of these nets can collect approximately 40 gallons of water each day. [10]When the fog develops, droplets of water are trapped in the nets and then flow down the nets into a trough. [11]From the troughs, the water drains through filters into a series of underground tanks. [12]The water is then piped to a 25,000-gallon storage tank, where it is chemically treated to kill disease-causing organisms. [13]Finally, the water flows to individual households, just as in traditional water systems. [14]This collection system can supply as much as 2,500 gallons per day, enough for the entire community to drink, wash, and water small gardens.

[15]The water is not only clean, but far less expensive than water delivered to the area. [16]Moreover, it is collected at no apparent cost to the environment. [17]It is likely that this system could be successfully implemented in other areas around the world with similar environmental conditions and economic constraints. [18]Researchers are investigating how this new water collection system could be adapted for noncoastal regions as well.

(Data from *Newsweek*, 18 October, 1993, and *Life*, November 1993)

1. As it happens, this passage and the passage in Task One each contain almost the same number of sentences, but this passage has three paragraphs rather than four. Why?

2. Another difference from the passage in Task One is that this passage contains a process description in paragraph 2. Make a sketch of the process.

3. What is the predominant verb tense used in sentences 6 through 14? Why is this?

4. Underline the instances of passive voice in paragraph 2.

5. In sentence 6 we have *is now being tested*. Why is the progressive used here? Is *being* appropriate?

6. Underline the adverbs in paragraph 2. How many of them are midposition adverbs?

7. Identify the two *this* + summary word phrases in the text. Where do they occur in the paragraph? Does this placement tell us anything?

8. How is the solution introduced?

Language Focus: Verbs and Agents in the Solution

In most technical solutions, it is necessary to describe a process. In the passage above, the explanation of how the water is collected provides this necessary information. We have looked at adverbs in process descriptions; it is now time to turn to verbs.

Passive Voice

The passive voice often plays an important role in process descriptions. We can see why in the following simple illustration. Look at these brief notes.

specimen—analyzed in the lab
results—recorded
report form—completed and sent to physician

We could turn these notes into instructions.

Analyze the specimen.
Record the results.
Complete a report form and send it to the physician.

These four activities are listed so that somebody can complete the task. Imperative forms are therefore used to indicate these necessary steps.

However, if we are interested not in explaining to someone how to complete a task, but in explaining *how the system works*—as in a process—we would more likely write:

> The specimen is analyzed in the lab. The results are recorded. A report form is completed and then sent to the physician.

Notice that each sentence now starts with a reference to a particular stage in the process:

the analysis stage,
the results stage, and
the reporting stage.

Notice how the focus on the stages is lost if the active is used.

> The technician analyzes the specimen in the lab. The technician records the results. The technician completes a report and then sends it to the physician.

Of course, there may be some occasions when the agents are an important part of the process.

> Technician A analyzes the specimen in the lab. Technician B records the results. Technician C completes a report and then sends it to the physician.

But this now looks like a job specification or duty roster. If information about the agent is important—which is uncommon—it would be better to describe the process in the following way.

The specimen is analyzed in the lab by technician A. The results are recorded by technician B. A report form is completed and then sent to the physician by technician C.

According to research studies, using *by* + a *human agent* is fairly uncommon in formal academic writing, except when describing the history of the field, as in:

The theory of transformational grammar was first developed by Noam Chomsky.

In fact, we are more likely to find *by* + *process*.

The chances of finding oil are often estimated *by seismic survey*.

Measurements can be made more accurate *by temperature control*.

Task Three

The *by* + *process* statements just given provide no details. Sometimes further information is useful. Expand as many of the following as you can. In other words, make the statements more informative by replacing the noun phrase with one or more verb phrases. Here is an example.

Teaching can be improved by in-service training.

Teaching can be improved by asking teachers to attend a range of short courses throughout much of their careers.

1. The spread of infectious diseases can be controlled by vaccination.

2. Pure water can be obtained by distillation.

3. Contact among researchers at different sites can now be maintained by E-mail.

4. Possible harmful effects of drugs can be reduced by tests.

5. One class of rocks is formed by sedimentation.

6. The area of a circle can be found by calculation.

7. Information on political preferences can be obtained by polling.

8. Cultures are partly preserved by ceremony and ritual.

9. Sequences of events at archaeological sites can be established by stratification.

10. Changes in land use can be detected by remote sensing.

In the "Clouds and Fog" passage in Task Two there were no occasions where the author (Chris) linked two or more passives together in the same sentence. Often, however, this may be required. Consider the simple case of the following nine sentences.

1. A specimen is collected.

2. The specimen is labeled.

3. The specimen is analyzed.

4. The results are recorded.

5. A report form is completed.

6. The report is dispatched.

7. The report is read.

8. The report is acted upon.

9. The report is filed.

Obviously, in this case, these nine sentences do not—as they stand—make a good process description. Rather than writing:

The sample is cleaned. The sample is dried. It is weighed.

We would prefer something like:

First, the sample is cleaned, dried, and weighed.

or:

The sample is cleaned, dried, and then weighed.

Task Four

Rewrite the nine sentences as a short process description. Use *first, then, next, finally,* etc. as you wish.

Before you start you should note that putting verbs together in this way can sometimes lead to an unfortunate ambiguity. How are the following ambiguous, and what can you do about it?

1. The liquid is collected and kept for 24 hours.
2. The sample is collected and stored in a sterile container.
3. In consumer research, individuals are selected and interviewed by telephone.

Change of State Verbs

So far we have emphasized the use of the passive voice in process descriptions. Part of the reason for this is that we have until now concentrated on processes that involve human action. There are, however, many natural processes that take place outside of human intervention. Such processes usually require the active voice, especially if their description employs verbs that indicate a change of state, such as *expand, rise, cool,* and *form.* Here are some examples.

The Sun *rises* in the east and sets in the west.
Most metals *expand* and *contract* with variations in temperature.
The beam *fractures* when the load on it becomes too great.
Tropical storms *can form* only in areas of high humidity and temperature. First, the warm sea *heats* the air above its surface. The warm, moist air then *rises* above the sea, creating a center of low pressure.

Now notice that scholars often use active verbs of this kind to make generalizations about human society.

When demand *increases*, prices are likely to *rise*.

Can you think of some other examples?

Causes and Effects

The last example sentence given is a cause-and-effect statement. Such statements can take many forms. Here are a few.

An increase in demand is likely to cause a rise in prices.
Increases in demand usually lead to price increases.
Demand increases; as a result, prices tend to rise.
Increases in price are often caused by increases in demand.

In the two longer texts we have examined in this unit, the authors described some causal relationships. Can you identify them here?

The databases are those established by the major abstracting and indexing services, such as the ISI indexes and Medline, which are predominantly located in the United States. As a result, these services have tended to preselect papers that (*a*) are written in English and (*b*) originate in the northern hemisphere. For these two reasons, it is probable that research in languages other than English is somewhat underrepresented.

When the cold air from the Pacific Ocean's Humboldt current mixes with the warm coastal air, a thick, wet fog, called *caman-chaca* by the Andes Indians, forms along with clouds.

Alternatively the authors could have written:

These services have tended to preselect papers that (*a*) are written in English and (*b*) originate in the northern hemisphere, *thus causing* research in languages other than English to be somewhat underrepresented.

The cold air from the Pacific Ocean's Humboldt current mixes with the warm coastal air, *resulting in* the formation of clouds and a thick, wet fog, called *camanchaca* by the Andes Indians.

Such -*ing* clauses of result can be particularly useful in writing a problem-solution text.

Language Focus: -*ing* Clauses of Result

As an alternative to using sentence connectors such as *therefore* and *as a result*, causal relationships can also be expressed by -*ing* clauses of result:

A. The magma flows into the pores of the rocks; as a result, the rocks rupture.
The magma flows into the pores of the rocks, *thereby causing* them to rupture.

B. A current is sent through the material. As a result, the electrons are polarized.
A current is sent through the material, *polarizing* the electrons.

Sometimes writers also use a preliminary subordinate clause to set the scene for the process:

C. When the piston is drawn upward, the air below rises. This causes the pressure to fall.
When the piston is drawn upward, the air below rises, thus causing the pressure to fall.

Subordinate clause (optional)	When the piston is drawn upward,
Main clause	the air below rises,
(thus/thereby) -*ing* clause	thus causing the pressure to fall.

This structure is particularly useful in problem-solution texts, because it can be used to express the next step in the process, a resulting problem, or a resulting solution. Here is a simple example.

Process: Prices rise, thus leading to a drop in demand.
Problem: Prices rise, thus increasing the chance of hyperinflation.
Solution: Prices rise, thus increasing earnings that can then be
  reinvested in the enterprise.

Task Five

Read the following sentences containing *-ing* clauses of result.
Would you expect to find these sentences in the problem, process, or
solution part of a text? Discuss your decision with a partner. There
is certainly room for disagreement on some of them.

1. The databases tend to preselect papers published in English,

   thus underrepresenting research published in other languages.

   _____

2. The warm moist air rises above the surface of the sea, creating

   an area of low pressure. _____

3. The cold air from the Pacific Ocean mixes with the warm

   coastal air, forming fog and clouds. _____

4. The system can collect as much as 2,500 gallons per day, thus

   providing a cheap and environmentally friendly supply for a

   small community. _____

5. The laser light forms an EM field, thereby slowing the vibra-
   formal

   tion of the atoms. _____

6. When manufacturing output falls, demand for business loans

   lessens, leaving the banks with a strong lending capacity.

   _____

7. In fact, sustainable development would require industry to re-

   duce both pollution and resource use, thus creating excellent

   opportunities for stimulating technical innovation.

   _____

8. With the advent of modern heating systems, the humidity levels inside buildings have fallen, causing antique wooden furniture to shrink and crack. ⎯⎯⎯⎯⎯

Task Six

Combine the ideas presented in each set of sentences, using an -*ing* clause of result. Work together in groups.

1. Sustainable development would require industry to reduce pollution output and resource use; as a result, technical innovation will be stimulated. *[handwritten: stimulating]*
2. The male *E. inconstans* performs an elaborate dance; the result is that the female is attracted. (*E. inconstans* is a small fish common in the waters of the Great Lakes region and Canada.)
3. The computer viruses infect executable files; as a consequence, the host computer is damaged when the executable is run.
4. The carcinogenic substances are extracted from the soil; hence, the soil is left uncontaminated.
5. Countries sign treaties on the use of "free resources," such as air and ocean fish. Serious ownership questions arise; therefore, it is difficult to enforce any agreement. *[handwritten: making it difficult]*

Task Seven

Now write a process description of your own choice. If possible, choose a topic that you can later incorporate into a full problem-solution text.

Language Focus: Indirect Questions

In one important sense, this unit has been about formulating questions (problems) and evaluating the answers to those questions (evaluations). For example, if we look back at two sentences in the text in Task One, we can see two examples of this.

4. It is not clear, however, whether such high percentages for English provide an accurate picture of languages chosen for publication around the world.

16. Until such time, nonnative speakers of English will remain uncertain about how effective their publications are in their own languages.

You probably noticed that in both cases the writer has opted to use an *indirect* question rather than a *direct* question. As you know, indirect questions follow the standard word order (the subject followed by the verb). They do not require that the subject and the verb be inverted, as in a direct question. Indirect questions also end with a period rather than a question mark. Here is a simple example.

Direct question: What time is it?
Indirect question: He asked what time it is/was.

The main difficulty in using indirect questions involves remembering that the *subject and verb should not be inverted* in an indirect question. Both research and experience suggest that *not inverting* is learned relatively late. Presumably, the use of a "question word" may automatically trigger the inversion. As a result, even native speakers may *incorrectly* produce:

It is unclear what will be the price of oil next year.

or

It is unclear what will the price of oil be next year.

rather than *correctly* produce:

It is unclear what the price of oil will be next year.

Task Eight

The verb *to be* is missing from the following statements. Insert it in the correct position for each. As you do so, note the typical language of indirect questions.

1. The question remains whether it possible to teach people to become effective instructors.

2. Current studies provide little information on how this policy being implemented in rural areas.

3. We need to know what students required to do when they write term papers.

4. There is some question as to whether the acquired skill then transferred to other contexts.

5. It has not been determined how these policies likely to affect small businesses.

6. It might also be of interest to investigate to what extent persistence a major factor in graduate student success.

7. Another issue raised by this study is whether and to what extent the economy subject to political developments elsewhere.

8. Without further research, conflicting opinions about which of the strategies the optimal one will continue.

Indirect questions have a number of functions in academic writing; for example, they can be used in explaining purpose.

A questionnaire was distributed to determine whether . . .

However, perhaps their most important use has been illustrated in Task Eight. They are often used to "problematize" issues, cases, phenomena, statements, and so on. For this reason, they are particularly common in problem-solution texts, first as one way of introducing the problem, and second as one way of offering a (critical) evaluation of the solution. In Task Nine you will have an opportunity to use indirect questions.

Although we have stressed indirect questions as a way of introducing or discussing problems, we do not want to imply that this is the only way. In some cases, direct questions may be possible.

However, is the data reliable?

Keep in mind, however, that you should limit your use of these in academic writing, as we stated in Unit One.

Another common way to introduce a problem is to use an adversative sentence connector, such as *however* or *nevertheless*. Here are some examples. Notice how each of these is somewhat negative.

However, this system/process/idea has its problems.
Nevertheless, few solutions have been found to . . .
Despite this, little progress has been made in . . .
However, there remains the issue of reliability.
Even so, researchers still have to find a way to make this vaccine available at a reasonable cost.

Task Nine

We interviewed a student about a current research project she was engaged in. Elly Choi is investigating the possibility of determining the points at which goods are damaged in processing, packaging, and shipping. Her advisor suggested that she begin her investigation by looking at the fruit industry. She has done considerable research on this topic and is ready to present her preliminary results to her professor. Write up Elly's report for her. Use a problem-solution text format. We have underlined sections that are written too informally for her report. Be sure to include a title.

Chris Feak: Why is this topic of interest?

Elly Choi: In the United States, bruised or damaged fruit will not be purchased by consumers. Bruising occurs at various times during the packing/shipping process. <u>We need to know</u> when the damage occurs in order to provide consumers with a quality product.

CF: What has been done so far?

EC: Information about the packing/shipping process can be obtained by using an artificial electronic fruit that goes through the process along with the fruit for consumption. Electronic fruits have been developed by Bosc and Jonathon (1988), Bartlett and Pippin (1989), D'Anjou and Cortland (1993). These devices were designed to transmit impact information *immediately*.

CF: Is there anything wrong with these prototype fruits?

EC: For one thing, these electronic devices were not sensitive enough to record the small, but frequent, bumps on the conveyor belt; thus, the data received was incomplete. For another, the noise produced by the machinery in the packing plants (where most of the bruising data is generated) interfered with the transmission of data; the data was, therefore, unreliable.

CF: What will you suggest?

EC: There are a bunch of options, but maybe this is the best. I think an electronic fruit that contains 256 bytes of RAM, 512 bytes of ROM, an 8 channel analog-digital converter, and a real time clock is the answer. It is important to store the data during the process and then download it later. If this is done, the specific bruises and damage can be correlated with the time and place each occurred.

CF: What are the problems with this solution?

EC: Well, I think . . . (Alas, the recorder ran out of tape at this point!)

Task Ten

Read the following short problem-solution texts. What differences do you detect between a and b? (Think of such matters as length, audience, amount of background knowledge assumed, amount of detail in each part of the problem-solution text, use of examples, etc.) Which text do you prefer? Why?

a. All people need to eat, and they eat a variety of foods—rice, fruits, vegetables, and meat. However, the problem is that sometimes people can become ill after eating spoiled or contaminated food. Each year millions of people become sick or even die. Meat can be particularly dangerous because it is difficult to determine whether it has been contaminated by simply looking at it. Fruit and vegetables at least have obvious signs of spoilage. One solution to this problem is to slow the process of spoilage by irradiation. Irradiated food lasts longer, tastes better, and in some cases may be cheaper. Since irradiated foods are completely safe, consumers now need to be convinced to buy them.

b. Each year millions of people suffer from foodborne illnesses.

Some health problems and even death can result from eating either spoiled fruits and vegetables or contaminated meat. Although in many countries strict governmental guidelines must be followed by meat producers, experts estimate that in the United States, for example, more than half the poultry sold to consumers is contaminated with *salmonella*. Some pork may harbor *trichinella*. For the last three decades, much research in food science has focused on whether it might be possible to eliminate potentially harmful bacteria before meat is sent to market. Many possibilities have been investigated, but one of the most promising is irradiation. Irradiation is a process that kills many harmful bacteria that cause spoilage, without affecting the food itself. As a result, irradiated food does not spoil as quickly as unirradiated food and also tastes better for a longer period of time. Food safety specialists agree that if irradiation were used, there would be a dramatic decrease in the rate of foodborne illnesses and deaths from eating contaminated food. Food costs might even be lower because the costs of spoilage would be reduced. While irradiation is being used on a relatively small scale, there is some public concern over its safety. It remains to be seen whether this revolutionary process can be implemented on a wide-scale basis.

Task Eleven

Write your own problem-solution text that includes a process description and, if possible, a definition.

Unit Four
Data Commentary

In many writing assignments, there comes a place where graduate students need to discuss data. Typically, the data is displayed in a table, graph, figure, or some other kind of nonverbal illustration. This data may be incorporated in the main text or attached as an appendix. We have called these writing subtasks *data commentaries*.

✰ Strength of Claim

Like many other aspects of graduate student writing, data commentaries are exercises in positioning yourself. There are, as a result, both dangers and opportunities. One danger is to simply repeat in words what the data has expressed in nonverbal form—in other words, to offer description rather than commentary. An opposite danger is to read too much into the data and draw unjustified conclusions. The art of the matter is to find the right strength of claim for the data and then order your statements in some appropriate way (such as from the more significant to the less significant). In most cases, this means moving in a general-specific direction (see Unit Two).

Task One

Working with a partner, put the following sentence variations in order from 1 (strongest claim) to 6 (weakest claim). Some disagreement is reasonable.

Deregulation of the U.S. banking industry _____ the 1989–91 banking crisis.

↗ hedging

2 a. contributed to *↖ participate*
1 b. caused → *result*
5 c. may have contributed to
4 d. was probably a major cause of
(2)3 e. was one of the causes of
6 f. might have been a small factor in

77

It is not easy to predict precisely what you might need to do in a data commentary, but here are some of the more common purposes.

• Highlight the results.
• Assess standard theory, common beliefs, or general practice in the light of the given data.
• Compare and evaluate different data sets.
• Assess the reliability of the data in terms of the methodology that produced it.
• Discuss the implications of the data.

Typically, of course, a data commentary will include more than one of these elements.

Task Two

Look over table 5, read the data commentary, and then answer the questions.

[handwritten: *definition*]
[1]A computer virus is a program that is specifically and maliciously designed to attack a computer system, destroying data. [handwritten: *general → specific*] [2]As businesses have become increasingly dependent on computer systems, concern over the potential destructiveness of such viruses has also grown. [3]Table 5 shows the most common modes of [handwritten: *direct to table*] infection for U.S. businesses. [handwritten: *textual*] [4]As can be seen, in the majority of [handwritten: *4 = Highlight 5.*] cases, the source of the virus infection can be detected, with disks being brought to the workplace from home being by far the most significant (43%). [5]However, it is alarming to note that the source [handwritten: *raising a issue*] of nearly 30% of viruses cannot be determined. [6]While it may be possible to eliminate home-to-workplace infection by requiring [handwritten: *6 Disscuss the implications*] computer users to run antiviral software on diskettes brought from home, businesses are still vulnerable to major data loss, especially from unidentifiable sources of infection.

1. Where does the data commentary actually start?

2. What are the purposes of sentences 1 and 2?

3. Do you consider this commentary a problem-solution text?

TABLE 5.   Means of PC Virus Infection in U.S.
Businesses

Source	Percentage
Disks from home	43%
Electronic bulletin board	7%
Sales demonstration disk	6%
Repair or service disk	6%
Company, client, or consultant disk	4%
Shrink-wrapped application	3%
Other download	2%
Disk from school	1%
Local area network supervisor disk	1%
Purposely planted	1%
Came with PC	1%
Undetermined	29%

© 1992 IEEE

4. What are some of the features of this text that make it an example of formal written English?

5. Which sentence contains the author's key point?

6. After Task One, we listed five common purposes for data commentaries. In which category does this one fall?

7. The author has chosen only to comment on percentages greater than 10%. Why? Do you think this is enough? If not, what would be a suitable additional sentence?

8. Undetermined sources constitute 29% of the total. In sentence 5, this is expressed as "nearly 30%." What do you think about this and these alternatives:
   a. over one-fourth of viruses
   b. 29% of viruses
   c. as much as 29% of all viruses

Structure of Data Commentary

Data commentaries usually have the following elements in the following order:

table 5

location elements and/or summary statements
highlighting statements
discussions of implications, problems, exceptions, etc.

Here is the data commentary again, with these elements marked.

Location + indicative summary

Table 5 shows the most common modes of infection for U.S. businesses. As can be seen, in the majority   Linking as clause
of cases, the source of viral infection can be detected,   Highlight 1
with disks being brought to the workplace from home
being by far the most significant. However, it is   Highlight 2
alarming to note that the source of nearly 30% of
viral infections cannot be determined. While it may be
possible to eliminate home-to-workplace infection by
requiring computer users to run antiviral software on
diskettes brought from home, businesses are still   Implications
vulnerable to major data loss, especially from
unidentifiable sources of infection.

We will now look at the first two of these elements in more detail.

Location Elements and Summaries

Many data commentary sections begin with a sentence containing these two elements. (See table 6.) The passive can also be used. (See table 7.) We bring two points to your attention here. First, note the consistent use of the present tense. This occurs because the author is talking about his or her present text. Second, in English the active forms are as appropriate as the passive versions. (However, in a number of languages it may not be natural to say that a graph or other inanimate object "reveals," "gives," or "suggests.")

Now notice that all the examples so far have been *indicative*. By

TABLE 6. Starting a Data Commentary

Location	Summary
a. Table 5 shows	the most common modes of computer infection for U.S. businesses.
b. Table 2 provides	details of the fertilizer used.
c. Figure 4.2 gives	the results of the second experiment.

TABLE 7. Passives in Starting a Data Commentary

Summary	Location
a. The most common modes of infection	are shown in table 5.
b. Details of the fertilizers used	are provided in table 2.
c. The results of the second experiment	are given in figure 4.2.

summarized
classified

this we mean that we have been told nothing yet about what the common modes of infection might be, which fertilizers were actually used, or what the results of the second experiment were. Alternatively, the writer could have given an *informative* summary; that is, the writer could have actually summarized the data.

a. Table 5 shows that home disks are the major source of computer viruses.*
b. Table 2 gives the ingredients of the chosen fertilizer—SP401.
c. Figure 4.2 suggests that the experimental results confirm the hypothesis.*

We have borrowed the terms *indicative* and *informative* from the major two-way classification of abstracts. Indicative abstracts merely indicate what kind of research has been done. Informative abstracts additionally give the main results. The parallel, we believe, is close.

---

*Notice the use of *that* in *a* and *c*. Sentences containing *that*-clauses do not easily go into the passive.

Language Focus: Verbs in Indicative and Informative Summaries

There are about a dozen verbs commonly used to make reference to nonverbal material. Some can be used with both types of summary statement. *Show* is one such verb.

Table 5 shows the most common modes of infection. (Indicative)
Table 5 shows that the most common source of infection is disks
    brought from home. (Informative)

Some verbs can be used with only one type of summary statement. *Provide*, for example, can only be used in an indicative summary.

Table 5 provides infection-source percentages.
not
Table 5 provides that the most common source of . . .

Task Three

Complete table 8. Write *Y* if the verb usage is possible and *N* if impossible. The first two have already been done.

Language Focus: Linking *as*-Clauses

So far, we have used sentences in which the reference to nonverbal data is either the subject or the agent in the main clause. However, a more common structure for introducing informative statements is the linking *as*-clause. Here are three examples.

As shown in table 5, home disks are the most frequent source of
    infection.
As can be seen in figure 8, infant mortality is still high in urban
    areas.
As revealed by the graph, the defect rate has declined.

These linking clauses (where *as* does not equal *since*) are exceptional in English grammar. In the passive, these clauses have no subjects. Compare sentences *a* and *b*.

What has in it   _what it says_

TABLE 8. Indicative and Informative Verbs

	Indicative	Informative
show	Y	Y
provide	Y	N
give	Y	
present	Y	
summarize	Y	Y
illustrate		
reveal		
display		
demonstrate		
indicate		
suggest		

a. As it has been proved, the theory may have practical importance.
b. As has been proved, the theory may have practical importance.

In _a_ there is a causal relationship between the _as_-clause and the
main clause. Because the theory has been proved, it may have practical importance. In _b_, the _as_-clause serves to announce or confirm.
   What has been demonstrated in _a_ and in _b_?
   Remember then _not_ to use subjects in passive linking _as_-clauses!

   Finally, using prepositions with this type of linking statement
can be tricky. Here are some of the main standard uses.

in   As shown _in_ table 3, . . .
from   As can be seen _from_ the data in table 1, . . .

by   As shown *by* the data in table 1, . . .
on   As described *on* page 24, . . .

Task Four   usually go with verb

Fill in the blank with an appropriate preposition.

1. As can be seen _____ in _____ figure 4, earnings have decreased.

2. As revealed _____ by _____ figure 2, the lightweight materials outperformed traditional metals.

3. As described _____ on _____ the previous page, there are two common types of abstracts.

4. As stated _____ in _____ Appendix B, *per in percent* or *kilometers per hour* is a Latin preposition that originally meant *through* or *by*.

5. As described _____ in _____ the previous unit, passives are common in process descriptions. *chapter*

6. As can be seen _____ by _____ a comparison of the two tables, household income is a more reliable predictor than level of education. *by* *comparing*

7. As is often the case *for/with/in* materials _____ of _____ this type, small cracks pose a serious problem.

8. As has been demonstrated *in/by* many similar experiments, these materials have many advantages.

Task Five

The following data commentary is missing references to the nonverbal data in table 9. Edit the commentary by (a) starting with a

TABLE 9. Strategies Used by Venezuelan Scientists When Writing in English ($N = 67$) @@@

Strategy	Percentage
Borrow phrases from English publications	26%
Write in Spanish and translate oneself	20%
Write in Spanish and employ a translator	18%
Write directly in English	15%
Outline in Spanish and then write in English	12%
Other strategies	9%

③ As revealed by table 9..., P8).

summary statement and (b) adding a suitable linking *as*-clause. Review the material presented up to this point before you begin.

① Table 9 shows strategies used by --- in English. ② Str. used by--- are presented in T9.

At least half of the scientists surveyed adopted writing strategies that involved the use of their first language. Moreover, only 15% p81. appear capable of writing directly in English. Overall, the figures would appear to suggest that most Venezuelan scientists have difficulties and frustrations when preparing papers for Anglophone audiences.

Tell the reader what your interpretation is.

Highlighting Statements

The central sections of data commentaries consist of highlighting statements. Highlighting statements are generalizations that you can draw from the details of the data display. We have already seen some examples in the texts that accompany Tasks Two and Three. Highlighting statements need good judgment. They are an opportunity to show your intelligence. In particular, they are an opportunity for you to demonstrate:

- that you can spot trends or regularities in the data,
- that you can separate more important findings from less important ones, and
- that you can make claims of appropriate strength.

So, do not

- simply repeat all the details in words,
- attempt to cover all the information, or
- claim more than is reasonable or defensible.

Qualifications and Strength of Claim

We said that highlight statements need good judgment. They also need good presentation of judgment. Thus, they have two requirements. One is the need to be cautious—and sometimes critical—about the data. As Skelton (1988) neatly observed, "It is important for students to learn to be confidently uncertain." The other requirement is to have the linguistic resources to express this caution. In this section, therefore, we deal with ways of qualifying or moderating a claim.

You have evidence

↑ real unreal word

Probability

can could poss. prob.

may might There are many ways of expressing probability in written academic

will would English. The simplest is the modal auxiliary. Notice how the claim

shall should progressively weakens in these three sentences.

must

A reduced speed limit *will result in* fewer highway injuries. *90%*

A reduced speed limit *may result in* fewer highway injuries. *35%*

A reduced speed limit *might/could result in* fewer highway injuries. *may/might overlap*

In these further examples, the phrases weaken in strength.

It is *certain* that

It is *almost certain* that

It is *very probable/highly likely* that

It is *probable/likely* that   a reduced speed

It is *possible* that   limit will result in

It is *unlikely* that   fewer injuries.

It is *very unlikely/ highly improbable* that

Don't overuse be ✓

There is a *strong* possibility that
There is a *good* possibility that
There is a *definite* possibility that } a reduced speed limit will result in fewer injuries.
There is a *slight* possibility that
There is a *remote* possibility that

will / should

Distance

Distance is another way of removing yourself from a strong—and possibly unjustified—claim. Compare these sentences.

Consumers *have* less confidence in the economy today than 10 years ago.

Don't overuse "seem".

Consumers *seem to have* less confidence in the economy.

Consumers *appear to have* less confidence in the economy.

use "appear"

It would seem/appear that consumers have less confidence in the economy.

It seems likely to

An alternative strategy is to distance yourself from the data by showing in some way that it is "soft." Here are a few examples.

tentative (no hard data)

On the limited data available,
In the view of some experts,
According to this preliminary study, } a lower speed limit may reduce highway fatalities.
Based on informal observations made by highway patrol officers,

Generalization

The classic verb for qualifying (or defending) a generalization is the verb *tend*. *it tends to be*

Consumers *have* less confidence in the economy.
Consumers *tend to have* less confidence in the economy.

seem to ... (+ a specific period of time)

Another way to defend a generalization is to qualify the subject.

Many consumers have less confidence in the economy.
A *majority of* consumers have less confidence in the economy.
In most parts of the country, consumers have less confidence in
the economy.
Consumers *in most income brackets* have less confidence in the
economy.

A third alternative is to add exceptions. "bald" generalizations
as precise as you can

With the exception of		a few oil-rich states, national economies
Apart from	}	in Africa are not likely to improve
Except for		greatly over the next decade.

Weaker Verbs

Finally, claims can be reduced in strength by choosing a weaker
verb. At the beginning of this unit, we compared the following.

A
Deregulation *caused* the banking crisis. (stronger)

B
Deregulation *contributed to* the banking crisis. (weaker)

Task Six

Underline the verb making the weaker claim.

1. The results indicate/establish that there is a link between
   smoking and lung cancer.

2. Table 9 suggests/shows that Venezuelan scientists may need
   help with writing English.

3. The latest series of experiments question/undermine much previous research.

4. The results given in figure 4 validate/support the second hypothesis.

5. The quantities displayed in the table have been as-
   sumed/shown to be about 98% accurate.

6. The test results create/suggest a basis for product modification.

7. Changes in ambient temperature may have influenced/ distorted the test results.

8. In their earlier work, they failed/neglected to take ambient temperature into account.

9. As can be seen from table 3, the new tax laws have encouraged/stimulated industrial investment.

[handwritten: similar or overlap]

10. Figure 12 depicts/clarifies the genetic relationship.

[handwritten: not clear case]

Combined Qualifications

[handwritten: "sweeping" generalization — no enough evidence]

Often, of course, several types of qualification are combined in order to construct a defensible highlighting statement. Here is an example. We start with a *big* claim!

The use of seat belts prevents physical injuries in car accidents.

Now see what happens when the following qualifications are added.

prevents → reduces   (weaker verb)
reduces → may reduce   (adding probability)
+ In some circumstances   (weakening the generalization)
+ certain types of injury   (weakening the generalization)
+ According to simulation   (adding distance)
   studies

So we now have:

According to simulation studies, in some circumstances the use of seat belts may reduce certain types of physical injuries in car accidents.

This sentence is a nice example of the writer being "confidently uncertain." (Of course, you also need to beware of excessive qualification since this may result in your saying almost nothing.)

Task Seven

Now, see what you can do with any *four* of the following. Make the
sentences academically respectable and defensible.

At certain point in life, can be   could be ; might be
1. Physical attraction is important for marital happiness. *is an important*
may be   *factor for...*

(In may case 2. Economic sanctions are ineffective.   *"Somewhat"*
In some circumstance   *not always (less)*
In general, 3. Alcohol causes people to become violent. *cause "certain" people*
can, may   *instead of : "some"*
may contribute to
4. Passive smoking causes cancer.
may be

5. Recycling is the best solution to the waste disposal problem.
one of the ↗   is "arguably the best - ...
(major)
In some person 6. Physical exercise lessens the severity of depression.

It's often 7. Great novels do not make great films.
not the case that
always , necessarily , guarantee
So 8. Private schools provide a better education than do public
schools.

Under certain circumstances
General speaking
A general view among people is that.. **Organization**

Highlighting statements are usually ordered from general to specific. In other words, major claims are followed by minor claims. We
saw this pattern, for example, in the short commentary on the Venezuelan scientists in Task Five.

However, decisions about organization become more complex with
comparative data. Consider the following case. You are taking a
graduate course in the social sciences. You have been studying differences in parental behavior with regard to their adolescent children. Your instructor suggests that, contrary to popular belief,
American parents may be stricter with their teenage sons than they
are with their daughters. You are given table 10, which is based on a
survey conducted among suburban families in a midsize Midwestern
U.S. city, and asked to prepare for the next class a short commentary on the main findings.

TABLE 10. Percentage of Adolescents Reporting the
Listed Parental Restrictions on their Lives
(N = 200) @@@

	Girls	Boys
Limitations on		
Opportunities to go out at night[1]	56%	35%
Use of the family car[2]	15%	40%
Time of expected return[3]	30%	61%
Interference in		
Choice of friends[4]	19%	23%
Future education choices[5]	18%	52%
Spending of self-earned money[6]	12%	27%

[1] E.g., may only be allowed out two nights a week.
[2] E.g., may be allowed only to use the car on special occasions.
[3] Curfew is imposed; e.g., has to be back by 11 P.M.
[4] E.g., girls are dissuaded from going out with older men.
[5] E.g., persuaded to study for a professional degree in college.
[6] E.g., required to bank 50% of earnings.

Task Eight

Three students wrote the following incomplete data commentaries.
They include only the locations statements and the highlighting
sections. What are the differences among the three? Which do you
think makes the best highlight statements and why.

Student A   *report repeat data*

Table 10 shows the percentage of adolescents reporting parental restrictions on their lives. As can be seen, about one-fourth
of female adolescents reported parental restrictions on average
across the six categories. Restrictions were most common on
going out at night (51%) and fewest on expenditure of self-
earned money (12%). In contrast, 40% of the males reported restrictions on average across the six categories. Restrictions
were most frequent for curfews (61%) and fewest for choice of
friends.

Student B   girls/boys

Table 10 shows the percentage of adolescents reporting parental restrictions on their lives. As can be seen, boys tended to be more restricted than girls. Over the six categories, boys reported an average of 40% restrictions but girls only 25%. In fact, boys were more restricted in five of the six categories, the only exception being going out at night. In this category, 56% of girls reported restrictions, but only 35% of the boys did so.

Student C

Table 10 shows the percentage of adolescents reporting parental restrictions on their lives. As can be seen, overall, boys tended to be more restricted by their parents than girls. However, the real difference lies in the rank order of the restrictions. The top three categories for boys were curfew, post-secondary education choice, and use of the family car; for girls, going out at night, curfew, and choice of friends. Although choice of friends occupied third place for girls, it was reported least by male adolescents.

Language Focus: Qualifying Comparisons

There is another kind of qualification that can be usefully employed in data commentary. We can illustrate this by looking again at the data on parental restrictions in table 10.

We have already said that it may not be a good idea to simply repeat the data in words. Therefore, it may not be a good strategy to make a series of statements like the following:

Fifty-six percent of girls reported restrictions on going out late at night as opposed to 35% of boys.

A series of such statements seems to imply that the reader is unable to read the numbers.

Instead we might opt for statements like the following:

More girls reported restrictions on going out late at night than did boys.

Fewer boys reported restrictions on going out late at night . . .
Not as many boys reported restrictions on going out late at night.

One problem here is the vagueness of *more* or *fewer.* How much, for example, is more: 2% or 10% or 50%? We could state it more exactly.

Twenty-one percent more girls reported restrictions on going out late at night.

While this statement is somewhat acceptable, it fails to convey the full magnitude of the comparison that you are trying to express. Just looking at the difference between the two is not that informative. Some useful alternatives follow. Can you complete each sentence?

a. Almost exactly twice as many boys reported . . .
b. A marginally smaller percentage of girls reported . . .
c. Slightly over twice as many boys reported . . .
d. Close to three times as many boys reported . . .
e. Boys exceeded girls in the times they reported . . . by a ratio of 2.5 to 1.

The fact that you are indeed able to complete the sentences shows the usefulness of these expressions.

Task Nine

Now write a full data commentary for table 10. Begin with a location element plus summary. Choose whatever highlighting statements you want (you are, of course, free to construct your own). Students A, B, and C did not offer any *cautious* explanations of the results. When you write your commentary be sure to do so. Look back at the section on qualifications and strength of claim.

Task Ten

You should find table 11 particularly interesting—and encouraging. Examine the table and study the commentary. You should be able to analyze its organization by now.

TABLE 11. Years to Doctorate for Doctoral Programs at University of Michigan, Ann Arbor, for Students Entering in 1981–83

Division	U.S. Citizens/Permanent Residents			International Students		
	N	% Ph.D.	Median Years to Ph.D.	N	% Ph.D.	Median Years to Ph.D.
Biological and health sciences	335	54	5.7	88	61	5.3
Physical sciences and engineering	469	44	5.3	430	55	5.0
Social sciences	409	35	6.0	80	59	5.3
Humanities and arts	373	33	5.3	91	53	5.0
Education	141	30	5.7	12	50	4.0
Individual departmental	16	38	6.5	4	50	3.7
Overall	1,743	41	5.3	705	56	5.0

Source: Horace H. Rackham School of Graduate Studies, University of Michigan.

[1]Table 11 shows the number of years to complete a doctoral program for both U.S. and international students at a major research university. [2]As can be seen, international students on average complete doctoral programs in less time than U.S. students in all divisions. [3]The difference in years to completion ranges from a relatively low 0.3 years in physical sciences/engineering and humanities/arts to a high of 2.8 years in individual departmental programs. [4]The consistent difference in time to degree is not fully understood at present. [5]However, one key factor may be motivation. [6]Many international students have considerable external pressures, including sponsorship/scholarship restrictions, family obligations, and employer demands, which could influence the length of time it takes to earn a doctorate.

Here are the instructor's comments on the commentary. The instructor is a professor of comparative higher education. Mark the comments as reasonable (*R*) or unreasonable (*U*) and discuss your choices with a partner. If you find some comments reasonable, how would you edit the passage? There are no absolutely right or wrong answers here.

____ 1. In sentences 2, 3, and 4 you throw away the key finding that more rapid progress to degree *and* higher completion rates is consistently in favor of international students across all six divisions. You need to highlight this more.
____ 2. You need to stress that based on present knowledge, we can only *speculate* about the explanations. As it stands I find sentence 5 hard to interpret. Is it just your idea, or do you have any evidence for this claim?
____ 3. It is strange that you do not mention the English language factor. At least at first sight, this would seem to suggest that international students ought to be taking longer.
____ 4. Don't you think you ought to finish by suggesting ways of getting at the real causes of this striking phenomenon? Case studies? Interviews with faculty and students?

Concluding a Commentary

As we have seen, qualifications can be important in making highlighting statements. They can be even more so in the concluding parts of a commentary. These parts are diagrammed in table 12, in the order in which they typically appear.

TABLE 12.   Concluding a Data Commentary

Explanations and/or implications	Usually required
↓	
Unexpected results or unsatisfactory data	If necessary
↓	
Possible further research or possible future predictions	If appropriate

Task Eleven

Here is an extended version of the commentary on the Venezuelan scientists in Task Five. Label each sentence according to its function and underline the qualifying words or phrases. The first sentence label has been provided.

[1]At least half of the scientists surveyed adopted writing strategies that involved the use of their first language. [2]Moreover, only 15% appear capable of writing directly in English. [3]Overall, the figures would appear to suggest that most Venezuelan scientists have difficulties and frustrations when preparing papers for Anglophone audiences. [4]Given the well-known differences between scientific English and scientific Spanish (Salagar 1992), the heavy use of the latter is somewhat unexpected. [5]This phenomenon probably reflects a lack of confidence in English. [6]Nevertheless, all the findings need to be treated with some caution, since they are based on what scientists said they did, rather than on direct observations of their writing. [7]Case studies of actual writing practices (cf. St. John 1987 on Spanish scientists) would be one possible direction for further research.

1. Highlighting statement _____

2. _____

3. _____

4. Unexpected result _____

5. _____

6. _____

7. _____

As in the case of Task Eleven, the data you are working with may not be perfect. In other words, it could contain some anomalies; or there may be discrepancies between the actual findings and the expected ones. Additionally, there may be obvious limitations in the study for which the data were collected. If any of these problems or limitations exist, usually the best strategy is to make a comment about them. You should try to explain why these unexpected results or errors occurred. Think back to Gene in Unit One. As you may recall, Gene was faced with a problem concerning the validity of his data. By bringing the problem out in the open, Gene was able to present himself as a perceptive and intelligent social scientist.

Language Focus: Dealing with "Problems"

The following phrases may be helpful as you discuss imperfect data.

The difference between expected and obtained results	may be due to the problem that ---	the incorrect calibration of the instruments.
This discrepancy	can be attributed to	the small sample size.
The anomaly in the observations	can probably be accounted for by	a defect in the camera.
The lack of statistical significance	is probably a consequence of	weaknesses in the experimental design.
The difficulty in dating this archeological site	would seem to stem from	the limited amount of organic material available.

Now notice how *due to* is used in the following sentences. Only the first three uses are definitely correct.

1. The errors may be *due to* incorrect calibration of the instruments.

2. The errors may be *due to* the fact that the instruments were incorrectly calibrated.
3. The errors may be *due to* the instruments being incorrectly calibrated. *awkward*
4. The errors may be *due to* the instruments were incorrectly calibrated. *that*
5. The errors may be *due to* incorrectly calibrating the instruments.

Sentence 4 is incorrect, while 5 is doubtful. While *due to* can sometimes be followed by an *-ing* clause, sentence 5 is problematic because of the lack of a clear agent.

Notice that in the correct statements, the verb phrase is followed by a noun phrase. If necessary, as in sentence 2, a noun phrase like *the fact that* could be added, even though *due to the fact that* is considered awkward by some instructors. Nevertheless, sometimes this is the only solution.

Task Twelve

You are a teaching assistant for an introductory biology course with a total enrollment of 150. Exams are usually given in the evening to avoid losing valuable class time. Because some students have evening commitments, a makeup exam is always given. The professor has noticed a big discrepancy between the scores of the last regular exam and those of the makeup exam. Because you administered the last makeup exam, you have been asked to offer an explanation. You

TABLE 13. A Comparison of the Regular and the Makeup Exam

	Regular exam	Makeup exam
Average score	86	72
Time administered	Wednesday, 7:00 P.M.	Friday, 4:00 P.M.
Difficulty	average	average
Number of students	125	25
Proctor	professor	teaching assistant
Board examples	yes	considered unnecessary
Room environment	about 20°C	about 28°C

have prepared the data in table 13. Now write a data commentary, either as a formal report or as a personal memo to your professor.

Dealing with Graphs

So far we have only considered tables. Discussions of graphs essentially follow the same principles as those for tables with one major difference. Much of the vocabulary of commenting on graphs is quite different.

Task Thirteen

Look at the graph in figure 6 and the accompanying data commentary written by one of our students. We have, however, omitted certain words and phrases. Can you complete the passage? Work with a partner or in a group.

The observed and predicted CO_2 levels for 24 hours in a commercial building ___ *are given / shown* ___ in figure 1. The actual CO_2 concentrations were ___ *collected* ___

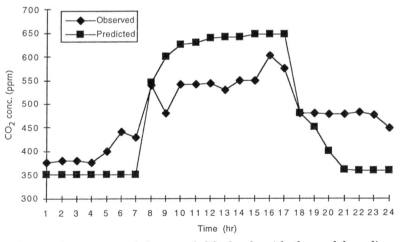

Fig. 6. Comparison of the actual CO_2 levels with the model predictions

directly from sites in the building by the CO_2 Trapping Method. The predicted concentrations were calculated by using one of the available indoor air quality models. In this case, the "fully stirred and conservative reactor with internal source model" _____ since it was assumed that the air was completely replaced and mixed with fresh air every hour, and there was no degradation.

_____ _Figure 6._ _____ shows that the predicted CO_2 concentrations increase sharply after 8 A.M. and ____ _decrese (drop/declire_ steeply after 6 P.M. This is because the CO_2 levels were ____ _assumed_ _____ to be dependent on the number of people in the building since people produce CO_2 as a result of respiration. However, the model overestimates the CO_2 levels during the occupancy periods (8 A.M. to 5 P.M.) and _____

_____

The lower CO_2 levels found in the occupancy period

_____

several factors, such as the presence of plants, which generate oxygen, while using CO_2. _____, the predicted levels are lower than the _____ during the vacancy period because the model assumed that nobody was in the building after 6 P.M. and that the air was fully mixed. In fact, there might be overtime workers in the building after 6 P.M., or the ventilation rate _____ during the vacant period. Although the "fully stirred and conservative reactor with internal source model" tends to overestimate or   underestimate _____ occupancy,

overall, it performs well with a coefficient of 0.9 (r = 0.9).

(Jiyoung Lee, minor editing)

Jiyoung has produced an excellent draft of a data commentary. But look at the last paragraph again. Do you have any suggestions for changes in tense usage?

Language Focus: Referring to Lines on Graphs

One feature of Jiyoung's data commentary is that she made little explicit reference to the lines on her graph. This occurs most often in cases of historical or technical data. As you know, graph lines have a special terminology. In fact, they have somewhat different terminologies depending on the discipline. We start with a typical social science graph providing historical data.

Look at figure 7. From the following list, choose a term that you think best describes each letter on the line of the graph.

upward trend	peak	low point	sharp rise
steep fall	rise	leveling off	fell off
remained steady	spike	increase	decline

Can you think of other terms that could be used?

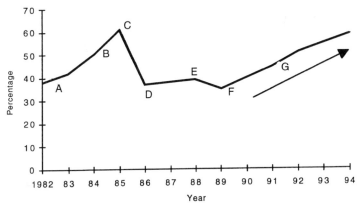

Fig. 7. Qualifying examination pass rates 1982–94 for mechanical engineering at Midwestern University @@@

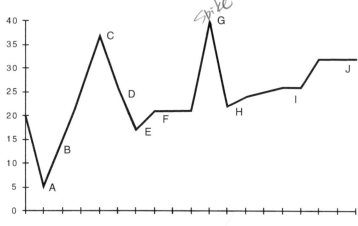

Fig. 8. Hard sciences graph @@@

Now look at a graph from the physical sciences in figure 8 and again choose a term that best describes each letter. Some terms may be used more than once.

minimum A   local dip/local minimum   local maximum
spike G   maximum/peak G   leveling off   J F
kink   linear increase

In what way are the terms for the physical sciences different?

Dealing with Chronological Data

The graph in figure 7 is the first nonverbal material we have given with a time dimension. Chronological data often present writers of data commentary with an organizational problem. On the one hand, writers want to follow the general-specific rule. On the other, they may want to respect the chronological order, that is, to start with the earliest and finish with the latest.

Task Fourteen

The sentences in this commentary expand on the information given in figure 7. They are not in the correct order. Rearrange them in an appropriate order. Place *1* in front of the first sentence, *2* before the second, and so on. Work with a partner if possible.

___ a. Some fluctuation is probably inevitable, since only less than 20 students took the qualifying exam each year.

___ b. As can be seen, the pass rate fluctuated quite widely.

___ c. From 1989 until the end of the period covered, pass rates have steadily climbed.

___ d. Figure 7 gives the qualifying examination pass rates in mechanical engineering at a U.S. research institution for the 1982–94 period.

___ e. In fact, the pass rate seems to be cyclical.

___ f. Other possible factors are the amount of research funding, the quality of the students themselves, and the priority given to doctoral funding.

___ g. Even so, the fact that 10 out of 15 students passed in 1985 probably caused the department to try and reduce its number of doctoral students the following year.

___ h. The years 1982–85 saw a rapid rise, followed by a steep fall in 1986 and then a low trough until 1989.

___ i. For instance, it reached a peak of 66% in 1985 and a low of 38% in 1989.

What can you conclude about how this data commentary is organized?

Language Focus: Prepositions of Time

Look back at the sentences in Task Fourteen and underline all the prepositions of time. Now study these alternatives.

From 1982 to 1985 the pass rates rose.
During the first four years, the pass rates rose.

The pass rate fluctuated *from* 1982 *to* 1994.
The pass rate fluctuated *throughout* the period.

The pass rate remained under 50% *from* 1986 *to* 1991.
The pass rate remained under 50% *until* 1991.

From 1985 on the level increased

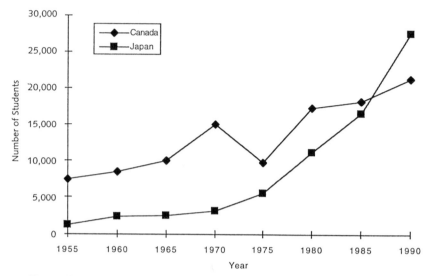

Fig. 9. Totals of Canadian and Japanese students in U.S. colleges and universities (at five-year intervals)

The highest pass rate occurred *in* 1985.
The highest pass rate occurred nine years ago.*

Task Fifteen

Write a suitable data commentary for figure 9. Would you like to speculate about future trends?

Task Sixteen

Write a data commentary from your own field of study based on data that you select.

---

*Of course the number of years ago depends on when you are writing! Here we assume 1994.

chronology is important

material Pre-R General
Russ specific

decolonize

Russian- Eurasian
sphere space
Sec
Int

Unit Five
Writing Summaries

Of all the writing tasks so far, summary writing may well be the one you are most familiar with. We make summaries of many different things, including conversations, lectures, and readings. Our summaries may be quite elaborate, or they may only involve one or two key words, depending on our purpose for writing them. These summaries of what others have written or said are our own *private* material. Most often we use this material for future reference. At the university especially, it can form an essential part of our *preparation* for an exam, a class discussion, or a term/research paper. In these situations, we are free to concentrate on what we think is important or interesting about the source.

Sometimes, however, writing a summary becomes a task in itself, such as when your instructor assigns a summary. In this case, you are given the opportunity to *display* your understanding of some material. This type of *public* summary is relatively common in graduate student writing and may be a foundation for other writing tasks.

In the first half of this textbook, you could successfully complete most of the writing tasks by relying either on information that you already possessed or on information that we provided. In the second half, we will pay more attention to writing that involves the use of sources. Unit Five deals with assignment summary writing. Unit Six deals with critiques of (or critical reactions to) source material. Finally, in the last two units, we move on to writing an entire research paper.

Writing an Assignment Summary

Assignment summaries can be extremely challenging to write. A good assignment summary has three principal requirements.

1. It should offer a *balanced* coverage of the original. (There is a tendency to devote more coverage to the earlier parts of the source text.)

2. It should present the source material in a *neutral* fashion.
3. It should *condense* the source material and be presented in the summary writer's *own* words. (Summaries that consist of directly copied portions of the original rarely succeed.)

paraphrase

Notice that we have not said anything about the length of a summary, because this will largely be determined by your instructor. Often, instructors will ask for a one-page summary of an article (or maybe a two-page summary of a book). They may also ask for a paragraph-length abstract (see Unit Eight) or even a minisummary of 1 to 2 sentences (as is typical of annotated bibliographies). Since the sample texts we provide here are quite short, we expect that the summaries you write will be half a page to a full page.

To do a good job, you must first thoroughly understand the source material you are working with. Here are some preliminary steps in writing a summary.

1. Skim the text, noting in your mind the subheadings. If there are no subheadings, try to divide the text into sections. Consider why you have been assigned the text. Try to determine what type of text you are dealing with. This can help you identify important information. *ask Q : why is that important?*
2. Read the text, highlighting important information or taking notes.
3. In your own words, write down the main points of each section. Try to write a one-sentence summary of each section.
4. Write down the key support points for the main topic, but do not include minor detail.
5. Go through the process again, making changes as appropriate.

Revisit

Task One

Read this adaptation of "Transformation of the Nile River Basin" and underline the information you think is significant and should be included in a summary. Next to each underlined section, briefly explain why you think the information is important. The first paragraph has been done for you. Then in as few words as possible, write in the margin what each paragraph is about.

Transformation of the Nile River Basin (adaptation)

The Egyptian landscape has been changing for centuries. One area which has undergone dramatic change over the last 7,000 years is the Nile River basin. One of the most notable aspects of this transformation is the year-round irrigation of land for agricultural purposes, rather than a strict reliance on the annual flood. Conversion to continuous irrigation, which began around 1500 and was limited only by the level of technology, led to improved agricultural productivity. This in turn contributed to an increase in the population of the area.

Large-scale conversion of agricultural land involving perennial irrigation began in 1800 with the availability of more modern technology. Water could be retained, raised, and distributed to summer crops with the aid of barrages* constructed on the Nile below Cairo and at sites on 30,000 km of new canals. Large dams were built on the Nile at Aswan in 1902, 1912, and 1933. The final transfor-

Reason for Highlighting

This is the topic of the passage.

technology change

The effect of the change in irrigation patterns is significant.

topic sentence

_____

_____

_____

_____

_____

*A barrage is a bank of earth or stones usually constructed over a river to provide water for irrigation.

mation to continuous irrigation was finished with the
completion of the Aswan Dam
in 1960. This full-scale change
brought about a major shift
and expansion in agriculture.
Cash crops such as cotton,
sugar cane, and vegetables
tended and still tend to be
produced at the expense of
subsistence crops.

Because Egyptians have
historically preferred to live
within or near the cultivated
land area, agricultural expansion has also had an impact
on the environment and liveli-
hood of the Nile population.
As the amount of land available for agriculture increased,
so did the population. Egypt's
population has increased from
2.5 million in the early 1800s
to 9.7 million in the late 1800s,
18.8 million in the 1940s, 37
million in the mid-70s, 46 million in 1984. The population is
projected to be 65 million by
the beginning of the next century. In 1907, urban dwellers
constituted only approx-
imately 17% of Egypt's population. By 1976, however, they
were 43% of the total. Recent
studies have indicated that
approximately 1–2% of Egypt's
arable land is lost annually to
human encroachment.

topic

transition
effect

(Steven M. Goodman, Peter Meininger, et al., eds. *The Birds of Egypt* (1989). Used by permission of Oxford University Press.)

Task Two

The "Nile" passage is fairly easy to summarize because it is factual, has three clear-cut sections, and follows a chronology. Take a look at some attempts at summarizing some of the details in the third paragraph. Which summary provides the right amount of detail? Explain your choice.

1. In the early 1800s the population of Egypt was 2.5 million. By the late 1800s it was 9.7 million. In the 40s the population reached 18.8 million; by the mid-70s it had reached 37 million. *Too many details* In 1984 the population was 46 million. In the year 2000 it is estimated that there will be 65 million Egyptians. One to two percent of Egypt's fertile land is disappearing annually as a result of the growth.

2. In the 1800s Egypt's population increased from 2.5 million to 9.7 million. In the 1900s it grew again, from 18.8 million in the 1940s to 46 million in 1984. By the next century, population *details* will be 1.5 times that in 1984. A result of this population growth is an annual 1–2% loss of agricultural land.

3. The Egyptian population has increased from 2.5 million in the early 1800s to 46 million in 1984. It is expected to reach 65 million by the year 2000. Along with this population growth, Egypt has also experienced a yearly 1–2% loss in the amount of fertile land. *truth?*

4. The Egyptian population has dramatically increased since the 1800s and is expected to continue to increase. A small percentage of agricultural land is lost each year because of the growth in population.

5. The Egyptian population in 1984 was nearly 20 times that in the early 1800s. By the next century, it should reach 65 million. Egypt is also losing agricultural land as a result of the population increase.

Now attempt your own summary of the third paragraph.

Task Three

Here is a passage written by one of our students. It is more difficult to summarize than the "Nile" passage because it is more argumentative. Read it and consider the parts that have been underlined because they were considered significant. Do you agree that the underlined sections are significant and for the reasons provided? Do you recognize the text-type?

Global Implications of Patent Law Variation

[1]A patent is an exclusive right to use an invention for a certain period of time, which is given to an inventor as compensation for disclosure of an invention. [2]Although it would be beneficial for the world economy to have uniform patent laws, each country has its own laws designed to protect domestic inventions and safeguard technology. [3]Despite widespread variation, patent laws generally fall under one of two principles: the first-to-file and first-to-invent. [4]The first-to-file principle awards a patent to the person or institution that applies for a patent first, while the first-to-invent principle grants the patent to the person or institution that was first to invent—and can prove it. [5]Most countries have adopted the first-to-file system. [6] However, the United States maintains a first-to-invent system,

This first sentence is a general definition. It may be safe to assume that your audience is already familiar with patents; thus you do not have to include it in your summary.

This is the main idea.

The classification of the two principles is important.

Ignore specific details about the different principles. The terms are self-explanatory.

It is important to point out that most of the world follows one system and the United States another.

despite obvious shortcomings.
[7]A result of countries employing different patent law principles is inconsistency of
patent ownership.

[8]Patent ownership is not
recognized globally. [9]On the
contrary, ownership may
change depending on the
country. [10]It is not uncommon
for an invention to have two
patent owners—one in the
United States and one in the
rest of the world. [11]This unclear ownership often has economic consequences. [12]If a
company is interested in using
a patented invention, it may
be unable to receive permission to do so from both patent
owners, which in turn may
prevent manufacture of a particular product. [13]Even if permission is received from both
owners, paying royalties to
both may be quite costly. [14]In
this case, if the invention is
useful enough, a company
may proceed and pass on the
added cost to consumers.

[15]International economic
tension has also been increasing as a result of differing
policies. [16]Many foreign individuals and companies believe
that they are at a serious dis-
advantage in the United
States with regard to patent
ownership because of the lo-

Include a description of the
problem surrounding variation
in patent laws.

Provide some support/
explanation for the problem,
but not all the details.

Describe this other problem
associated with differing patent principles.

gistical difficulties in establishing first-to-invent status. [17]Further, failure of the United States to recognize patent ownership in other countries is in violation of the Paris Conventions on Industrial Properties, which requires all member nations to treat all patents equally. [18]The conflict surrounding patents has prompted the World Intellectual Properties Organization (WIPO) to lobby for universality in patent laws. [19]WIPO maintains that the first necessary step involves compelling the United States to reexamine its patent principle, taking into account the reality of a global economy. [20]This push may indeed result in more global economic cooperation.

Provide some explanation, but not all the details.

Describe the action taken to solve the problem.

(Koji Suzuki, minor editing)

You may have realized that this is a problem-solution text. Label the significant parts of the text (refer back to Unit Three, table 4).

A preliminary summary of this passage *+ evalution* should contain the key elements: situation, problem, and solution. In the next step, these elements can be strung together to form the basis of a formal summary. Of course, special care has to be taken to ensure a logical flow of ideas. Here is a draft.

[1]Although it would be beneficial for the world economy to have uniform patent laws, each country has its own laws. [2]Despite widespread variation, patent laws generally fall under one of two principles: the first-to-file and first-to-invent. [3]Most countries have adopted the first-to-file system. [4]However, the United States maintains a first-to-invent system.

[5]A result of countries employing different patent law principles is inconsistency of patent ownership. [6]Patent ownership is not recognized globally. [7]This unclear ownership often has economic consequences. [8]International economic tension has also been increasing as a result of differing policies. [9]Further, failure of the United States to recognize patent ownership in other countries is in violation of the Paris Conventions on Industrial Properties. [10]The conflict surrounding patents has prompted the World Intellectual Properties Organization (WIPO) to lobby for universality in patent laws. [11]WIPO maintains that the first necessary step involves compelling the United States to reexamine its patent principle, taking into account the reality of a global economy.

This draft is perhaps a reasonable beginning. The writer has retained the important parts of a problem-solution text. Most of the sentences are short, as we would expect in a summary. However, this summary has three faults.

1. It is probably a bit too long. The original contains 399 words, and the summary contains 168. It could be condensed further without any loss of meaning.
2. It is written entirely in the words of the original, although no whole sections were borrowed. It is an example of plagiarism. Notice that sentence 1 in the summary is identical to the first highlighted part of the original, sentence 2 is identical to the second highlighted section, and so on.
3. It does not display a high level of understanding of the source *re—cast !* passage. While it does show that the writer can pull out important information, it does not convince the reader that the summary writer understands the information and how it is interrelated. *restate others' articles in a logical way*

Overall, this summary is fine as a set of personal notes, but it is too close to the original to be used as a written assignment.

Now, let us consider how this summary could be improved. One obvious approach would be to paraphrase the original. A paraphrase is a restatement (in your own words) of the ideas in the original. The most common strategy used to accomplish this involves replacing words in the source with synonyms and perhaps changing the grammar. Look again at the first sentence.

Cut. Although it would be beneficial for the world economy to have uniform patent laws, each country has its own laws.

A (paraphrase) of this could be

> Every country has unique patent laws, even though the world economy would be improved if they were consistent.

Is this paraphrase a reasonable representation of the original?

This method can often be successful, but if you do this sentence by sentence, you will most likely not demonstrate your full understanding of the passage. Another weakness is that the resulting summary is not original and would be considered plagiarism by many people. Simple synonym substitution is often not considered to be original work. Far more needs to be changed from the original source. A better but more difficult strategy for summary writing would be to carefully consider the elements you consider important, put the original away, and write down what you have understood. This may allow you to condense the ideas in the source even further.

When you write a formal summary of someone else's ideas, you should keep in mind the following guidelines. (Remember, if you are taking notes for yourself, direct copying is OK, but it is a good idea to indicate in your notes when you are directly copying.)

1. Always try to use your own words, except for technical terms.
2. Include enough support and detail so that the presentation is clear.
3. Do not try to paraphrase specialized vocabulary or technical terms.
4. Include nothing more than what is contained in the original. (Do not include your own comments or evaluation.)
5. Make sure the summary reads smoothly. Use enough transition devices and supporting detail. You do not want a collection of sentences that do not flow.

Problem — solution

Task Four

Read these two summaries and answer the questions that follow.

Draft Summary

¹Although it would be beneficial for the world economy to
have uniform patent laws,
each country has its own laws.
²Despite widespread variation,
patent laws generally fall under one of two principles: the
first-to-file and first-to-invent.
³Most countries have adopted
the first-to-file system. ⁴How-
ever, the United States maintains a first-to-invent system.
⁵A result of countries employing different patent law principles is inconsistency of
patent ownership.

⁶Patent ownership is not
recognized globally. ⁷This
unclear ownership often has
economic consequences. ⁸In-
ternational economic tension
has also been increasing
as a result of differing policies. ⁹Further, failure of the
United States to recognize
patent ownership in other
countries is in violation of the
Paris Conventions on Industrial Properties. ¹⁰The conflict
surrounding patents has
prompted the World Intellectual Properties Organization
(WIPO) to lobby for univer-

Rewrite Summary

inconsistency

¹Lack of consistency in the
world's patent laws is a serious problem. ² In most countries, patent ownership is
given to the inventor that is
first to file for a patent. ³However, the United States maintains a first-to-invent policy.
⁴In view of this, patent ownership can change depending on
the country. ⁵Multiple patent
ownership can result in economic problems; however,
most striking is the international tension it causes. ⁶The
fact that the United States
does not recognize patent
ownership in other countries,
in violation of the Paris Convention on Industrial Properties, has prompted the World
Intellectual Properties Organization (WIPO) to push the
United States to review its existing patent law principles.

U.S.

cause
problem

solution

sality in patent laws. [11]WIPO
maintains that the first necessary step involves compelling
the United States to reexamine its patent principle,
taking into account the reality
of a global economy.

1. How closely do the two summaries follow the five guidelines given on page 114? *draft* ↓↑

2. Does the rewrite summary present the main idea of the original text in Task Three? Is there adequate support and explanation?

3. Is the rewrite summary objective? *Yes*

4. Is it too long or too short? *no*

5. Has the writer of the rewrite used his or her own words? *Yes*

6. Is there anything missing from the rewrite summary? *reference — author name*

7. What changes were made from the draft summary to the rewrite? *precise*

8. Which vocabulary items were not paraphrased in the rewrite? Why? *WIPO — technical term* *first to file / Invent*

One important element is still missing from the summary. The source has not been provided. Since many of the summaries you write will be woven into your own original text, it is very important to identify at least the source author, if not the title as well. Here is one way to identify your source.

In his paper "Global Implications of Patent Law Variation," Koji Suzuki (1991) states that lack of consistency in the world's patent laws is a serious problem.

The following language focus provides some additional suggestions on how to begin your summary.

Language Focus: The First Sentence in a Summary

Most summaries begin with a sentence containing two elements: the source and the main idea. Notice the use of the present tense in the last three examples.

In Anthony Tyson's article "Mapping Dark Matter with Gravitational Lenses," _____.
               (main idea)

According to Yvonne Boskin in her article "Blue Whale Population May Be Increasing off California," _____.
               (main idea)

Young and Song's 1991 paper on fluoridation discusses

_____.
  (main topic)

Author Peter Bernstein in his book *Capital Ideas* states that
_____.   claims
  (main idea)   argues
                        maintains

Marcia Barinaga, in her article "Is There a Female Style in Science?" states that _____.
     argues   (main idea)
     maintains
     suggests
     claims

Although, in theory, summaries are supposed to be objective, this is not entirely true. A wide range of reporting verbs can be used in summary writing, many of which reveal the summary writer's personal attitude toward the source material. These evaluative verbs should be used sparingly in summaries. Notice how the evaluative verbs in the following examples allow the writer of the summary to convey his or her attitude.

Marcia Barinaga in her article "Is There a Female Style in Science?" *alleges* that men and women exhibit differences in the way they pursue science.

Marcia Barinaga in her article "Is There a Female Style in Science?" *assumes* that men and women exhibit differences in the way they pursue science.

Some reporting verbs are less objective than others. Can you identify which verbs in table 14 seem to be objective and which verbs tend to be evaluative? The first answer has been provided for you.

Language Focus: Nominal *that*-Clauses

In formal academic English, many reporting verbs are followed by a *that*-clause containing both a subject and a verb. Can you identify the verbs in table 14 that are not followed by *that*? List them here.

That-clauses have a variety of functions. In the following sentence, the *that*-clause is the direct object of the verb *states*.

Marcia Barinaga in her article "Is There a Female Style in Science?" states *that* men and women are indeed different.

In spoken English, *that*-clauses which function as direct objects are often omitted, as in the following example. Notice also that in this spoken English alternative the choice of verb is less formal.

In her article, Marcia Barinaga *says* there is a difference in the way men and women pursue scientific research.

You may have wondered why we have not said anything about the verb *mention* in the opening sentence of a summary. Notice that if you were to use *mention* instead of one of the other verbs suggested, you would greatly change the importance of the information following. → imply that is not main point
degreat the importance

TABLE 14.   Objectivity of Reporting Verbs

	Objective	Evaluative
describe	X	
discuss	X	
state	X	
present	X	
explain	X	
maintain	X	X
examine	X	X
affirm		X
argue		X
reveal	X	(X)
presume		X
assume	(X)	X
assert		X
contend		X
allege		X
claim		X
imply		X

(Handwritten annotations:)

ducation
e these } ☆ (describe, discuss)
ins most
equent

☆ present

Insist   claim   maintain

Ed
least
frequent
X affirm, argue, reveal, presume, assume, assert, contend, allege, claim, imply

X presume
X allege
X imply

(less than "presume")
between "state" & "claim"

standard term in evaluative

imply
infer

Anthro/Ling / Soc/Poli Sci
most fre: argue, claim, present, examine, discuss
least fre: presume, contend, allege, affirm

Marcia Barinaga in her article "Is There a Female Style in Science?" mentions that men and women exhibit differences in the way they pursue science.

How does this sentence compare to the first example presented in this language focus?

Mention is used for information that was most likely given without detail or support. The example sentence using *mention* makes it seem as if the difference between men and women is a minor point in the article. We suggest that you avoid using *mention* at all in summaries.

Task Five

Here are some introductory statements that students wrote for a summary of the "Nile" passage in Task One. Which, if any, would you prefer to have written? Why? Edit the weaker sentences.

1. Author Steven Goodman in "Transformation of the Nile River Basin" states that how the region has changed as a result of continuous irrigation. *states how or states that*

2. "Transformation of the Nile River Basin" by Steven Goodman claims that changes in irrigation have led to an increase in population. 不用文章当 S 来 claim

observes notes explains bias

3. According to "Transformation of the Nile River Basin," Steven Goodman suggests that the Nile River basin has been changed. *not complete*

4. Goodman in "Transformation of the Nile River Basin" mentions that irrigation has had an impact on the environment and the population.

5. In Goodman's "Transformation of the Nile River Basin," the Nile River basin has been transformed by the introduction of perennial irrigation. (*misleading*)

If you are summarizing another author's work as part of a longer paper, you may make a reference to your source material following the APA (American Psychological Association), MLA (Modern Language Association), or IEEE (Institute of Electrical and Electronics Engineers) or another style, depending on your field of study. The APA and MLA systems refer to a source similarly, by author and date. The following references are in APA style.

a. Goodman (1989) has found a correlation between the increase in agricultural fertility and the shift away from traditional crops.
b. A correlation between the increase in agricultural fertility and the shift away from traditional crops has been identified (Goodman, 1989).
c. In his recent study of the Nile River basin, Goodman (1989) established a correlation between the increase in agricultural fertility and the shift away from traditional crops. Goodman also noticed . . .

How does the citation in sentence *b* differ from sentences *a* and *c*?

For a thorough discussion of APA and MLA styles, see the *Publication Manual of the American Psychological Association* and *The MLA Handbook for Writers of Research Papers*.

In engineering, it may be more common to use reference numbers.

Photorefractive crystals may be useful in the development of high-speed electrical signals.[1]

If you are in engineering, check the journals in your specific area to learn more about documentation for that area of engineering.

Language Focus: Summary Reminder Phrases

- focus
- avoid plagarism

In a longer summary, you may want to remind your reader that you are summarizing.

The author goes on to say that . . .
The article further states that . . .
(author's surname here) also states/maintains/argues that . . .
(author's surname here) also believes that . . .
(author's surname here) concludes that . . .

In the second half of the paper, *(author's surname here)* presents . . .

In fact, you may want to mention the source author's name at three points in your summary—the beginning, the middle, and the end. In a short summary, it would be rather awkward to mention the author so frequently, and the text would not flow well if each sentence began with the author's name; however, in a longer summary, mentioning the author three times would be quite appropriate. When you do mention the author in the middle or end of the summary, be sure to use the surname only.

a cording to - ...
Goodman goes on to say . . .
Suzuki also believes that . . .

Some of the following linking words and phrases may be useful in introducing additional information.

additionally	in addition to
also	furthermore
further	moreover

The author *further* argues that . . .

Task Six

Here are some summary reminder sentences written by our students. Which, if any, of these would you prefer to have written? Try to improve the weaker sentences.

1. Harmon finally *states* says people are making a big fuss over the nuclear waste problem.

2. In addition, the *author's* article also discusses about the dangers of current disposal methods.

3. In Saleska's article, he also points out that low-level radioactive waste can be harmful.

4. Harmon concludes that current regulations need to be reexamined.

5. Saleska concludes about the current changes in regulations.

not specific

Task Seven

Here again is the summary of the Suzuki passage in Task Three. Would it be improved by adding a reminder phrase? Where would you insert it?

Summary

[1]In his paper "Global Implications of Patent Law Variation," Koji Suzuki (1991) states that lack of consistency in the world's patent laws is a serious problem. [2]In most of the world, patent ownership is given to the inventor that is first to file for a patent. [3]However, the United States maintains a first-to-invent policy. [4]In view of this, patent ownership can change depending on the country. [5]Multiple patent ownership can result in economic problems; however, most striking is the international tension it causes. [6]The fact that the United States does not recognize patent ownership in other countries, in violation of the Paris Convention on Industrial Properties, has prompted the World Intellectual Properties Organization (WIPO) to push the United States to review its existing patent law principles.

more like a point of view

according to suzuki

because

Task Eight

Read "Reducing Air Pollution" and try to determine the text-type. Then read the summaries that follow. Decide which of the summaries you like best. Write 1 to 2 sentences after each summary, explaining what you liked or disliked about each. Finally, discuss each of the summaries with a partner.

study — past
paper generation — present

generalization — present tense
tracing the development — This has been tested...
Talking about history — past tense
open to public & talk st alive, people still talk — present
it's under discussion now
~ perfect

Reducing Air Pollution in Urban Areas:
The Role of Urban Planners
Yasufumi Iseki

Recently, increasingly significant problems regarding energy use have emerged. Enormous amounts of pollutants are being emitted from power plants, factories, and automobiles, which are worsening the condition of the earth. This environmental degradation is a clear result of acid rain, increased levels of carbon dioxide (CO_2) in the atmosphere, and other forms of air pollution.

Acid rain and air pollution, for instance, are devastating forests, crops, and lakes over wide areas of Europe and North America. In fact, in Europe nearly 50 million hectares have been identified as damaged, representing 35% of the total forested area. In the United States, approximately 1,000 acidified and 3,000 marginally acidic lakes have been reported. Since the midcentury, CO_2 levels in the atmosphere have increased by 13%, setting the stage for global warming. As atmospheric temperatures rise, grain output may significantly decrease, making it more difficult for farmers to keep pace with the growth of population. In urban areas, air pollution is taking a toll on buildings and human health.

To reduce the amount of environmental damage in cities specifically, developed countries have devised technology to control the harmful emissions. However, as these countries already have an abundance of vehicles that continues to grow in number, the efficacy of these measures is diminished. Since cars and other vehicles create more air pollution than any other human activity, the most effective means to reduce pollution is to decrease the number of vehicles. A major shift away from automobile usage in urban areas may be possible with the aid of urban planning.

Summaries

1. According to Yasufumi Iseki, air pollution can be controlled through effective urban planning.

2. Yasufumi Iseki in "Reducing the Air Pollution in Urban Areas: The Role of Urban Planners" states that pollutants are worsen-

too much detail.

ing the condition of the Earth as a result of acid rain, increased levels of CO_2, and other forms of pollution. In fact, 35% of the total forested area in Europe has been damaged, and in the United States, approximately 1,000 acidified lakes and 3,000 marginally acidic lakes have been reported. Since the midcentury CO_2 levels have increased by 13%. Cars and other vehicles create more pollution than any other activity; thus, decreasing the number of vehicles is the most effective way to reduce pollution. This may be possible with urban planning.

3. Yasufumi Iseki states that because cars and other vehicles are the greatest single source of air pollution, a reduction in the number of vehicles in urban areas would be an effective approach to improving the urban environment. This reduction could be achieved through urban planning.

suggests   too strong

4. Yasufumi Iseki claims that urban planning can play a role in improving air quality in urban areas by prompting a shift away from heavy vehicle use. This will be difficult to achieve because of the overabundance of vehicles in developed countries.

Some Notes on Plagiarism

Plagiarism is best defined as a deliberate activity—as the conscious copying from the work of others. The concept of plagiarism has become an integral part of North American and Western European academic cultures. It is based on a number of assumptions that may not hold true in all cultures. One is a rather romantic assumption that the writer is an original, individual, creative artist. Another is that original ideas and expressions are the acknowledged property of their creators (as is the case with a patent for an invention). Yet another is that it is a sign of disrespect—rather than respect—to copy without acknowledgment from the works of published authorities.

Of course, borrowing the words and phrases of others can be a useful language learning strategy. Certainly you would not be plagiarizing if you borrowed items that are commonly or frequently used in academic English or that are part of common knowledge.

[handwritten: no] Paris is the capital of France.

[handwritten: no] An increase in demand often leads to an increase in price.

[handwritten: must cite] The results from this experiment seem to suggest that ... *[handwritten: not common knowledge]*

[handwritten: cite] These results are statistically significant.

But do not borrow "famous" phrases without at least putting them in quotation marks. Here, for example is a famous quotation by Louis Pasteur. It was originally in French.

Chance favors the prepared mind.

If you wanted to use this phrase, you should recognize its special status. We would encourage you to borrow standard phraseology from native speakers when appropriate, but not special expressions.

Task Nine

Here are some approaches to writing, beginning with a plagiarizing approach and ending with an acceptable quoting technique. Where does plagiarism stop? Draw a line between the last approach that would produce plagiarism and the first approach that would produce acceptable original work.

[handwritten: X] 1. Copying a paragraph as it is from the source without any acknowledgment.

[handwritten: X] 2. Copying a paragraph making only small changes, such as replacing a few verbs or adjectives with synonyms.

[handwritten: X] 3. Cutting and pasting a paragraph by using the sentences of the original but leaving one or two out, or by putting one or two sentences in a different order.

[handwritten: gray area In between] 4. Composing a paragraph by taking short standard phrases from a number of sources and putting them together with some words of your own. *[handwritten: patch job]*

5. Paraphrasing a paragraph by rewriting with substantial changes in language and organization, amount of detail, and examples. *[handwritten: It's still a good idea to do (Gordon, 1999)]*

6. Quoting a paragraph by placing it in block format with the source cited.

[handwritten: cite]

Task Ten

Complete your own summary of the *Nile* passage in Task One. Try to limit yourself to 150 words or less.

Task Eleven

Choose a short article or article passage from your field of study and write a summary.

Comparative Summaries

Comparative summaries are common in many graduate courses. They can be assignments on their own, part of a longer paper, or a response to an examination question. Comparative summaries can be more challenging to write than simple summaries, because they require you to analyze and use information from two or more sources rather than just one. In a comparative summary, you often need to infer and make explicit the relationships among your sources. Unlike a traditional summary, a comparative summary may not be an objective representation of the original sources. If you write a comparative summary in response to a question, you will use only material from the source that is *relevant* to the task.

Task Twelve

The following are questions from the fields of neurobiology, economics, and epidemiology. How would you approach each of these tasks? What do you think are the instructor's expectations?

1. What do Alkon and Farley believe the role of seratonin to be in memory? In what ways do they fundamentally differ? How are they similar?

2. How do Winder & Gori and Agran view the political implications of recent evidence regarding occupational cancers?

tough

3. Relate Kohl and Jaworski's 1990 article "Market Orientation: The Construct, Research Propositions, and Managerial Implications" to product and service quality. Consider the perspectives of Juran, Feigenbaum, Deming, and Crosby. What common themes emerge and how do they differ?

Construct a similar task for your own field of study. How would you plan to answer it? Be prepared to explain your task and plan in class.

Task Thirteen

In this task we return to a topic introduced in Unit Two—humor. Read the following two comparative summary *drafts* written in response to the following question on a recent take-home examination in psychology.

> Discuss Wilson (1979) and Ziv (1984) as they relate to the social function of humor. In what ways are they similar? How do they differ?

Which of the responses do you prefer? Why? How might the response you prefer be improved?

1. In *Jokes: Form, Content, Use, and Function,* Wilson states that humor has a variety of both personal and social functions. For example, it may be done to lower hostility levels, to rebel, or to raise sensitive issues. Regardless of the reason, the audience may choose whether to laugh. The broader, social function of joking is to simply maintain the status quo. People joke to reduce friction and anxiety as well as to ridicule others in a relatively safe way. Joking can be a way for minorities to release frustrations about being in less powerful positions. Wilson also notes that there is usually a pecking order or hierarchy in humor. Superiors joke about their subordinates. Those within a certain group joke about those outside the group. Joking is often directed at those in positions perceived as subordinate.

   Ziv, in *Personality and Sense of Humor* sees the social function of humor as one of control and maintaining or establishing rapport. Joking is a way to maintain social order. People joke about outsiders—people not in the mainstream. Jokes also arise when social norms have not been adhered to. People, therefore, act "appropriately" so as to not become the victim of a joke. Jokes are also a reflection of social hierarchy. People in "higher" positions joke about those in lower positions. While the former may freely joke about the latter, the latter may joke about the former only in private. For those in a "lower" position, then, humor is a way to relieve tensions and frustrations. Ziv goes on to say that joking can be a means of initiating and improving relationships with others. It is way of narrowing social distance. The inside jokes of a group are a part of the identities of the individual members.

2. Wilson and Ziv maintain that humor serves a social function. For one thing, jokes reveal the social hierarchy. The authors agree that superiors freely joke about those in lesser position. Subordinates, including minority groups can privately joke about those in "higher" positions in order to reduce tension and feelings of frustration. For another, humor is beneficial for a group. Although Ziv more clearly explains this point, Wilson would agree that joking about nongroup members can not only help unify a group but can also play a role in establishing individual identities.

While both Wilson and Ziv analyze joking in terms of relationships among individuals, Ziv has a somewhat broader view. Ziv argues that humor is a way to exert social control. Jokes frequently focus on situations where social norms have been broken. Therefore, in order to avoid becoming the victim of a joke, people tend to follow social conventions.

(Adapted from Neal N. Norrick, *Conversational Joking* [Indiana University Press, 1993])

Task Fourteen

Find two articles on the same topic. Write a comparative summary.

This paper is interesting in terms of.....
a through examination
stimulating

Unit Six
Writing Critiques

In Unit Five, we worked on writing descriptive and comparative summaries. In this unit, we extend this work to the writing of critiques. *Critique* is a French word that means a critical assessment (positive, negative, or a mixture of both). One common type of critique you may be familiar with is the film review in a newspaper. Critiques may have various structures, but the simplest is a short summary followed by an evaluation. This unit will concentrate on the evaluation portion.

In our experience, critique assignments are employed somewhat variously in U.S. graduate programs. Certain instructors—from a wide range of programs—use them on a regular basis; certain others almost never do. In some fields of study, critiques are a regular part of take-home examinations; in other fields, they rarely are. Instructors may assign critiques for several reasons:

1. To try and ensure that students actually do reading assignments
2. To assess the students' understanding
3. To try and develop habits of analytic reading in their students
4. To train graduate students to integrate the assigned reading with other readings they have done, especially by making comparisons
5. To give graduate students a better sense of the scholarly expectations in their chosen field

The first four purposes are similar to those we have already seen for summaries. The fifth is somewhat different. Summaries focus on an accurate account of the content of the original article. Critiques require that students also learn to express their evaluative comments within their field's accepted standards of judgment.

It is important that critiques be "fair and reasonable." Part of being "fair" means that criteria that are reasonable in one field should not be applied to another field where they would be unreasonable. For example, in terms of how precise a measurement needs

131

to be, psychology is not comparable to physics. Or, in terms of the expected size of an experimental group, research into language teaching methodology is not comparable to efforts to measure elementary school reading ability. The question of how "fair" criticism varies from one field to another is an issue that we will return to later.

We should also note at this stage that different fields are likely to impose different emphases on critiques. In the humanities, attention may focus on how "interesting" the arguments are; in the social sciences, on the methodology; and in the sciences and engineering, on the results and what they might (or might not) signify.

The final point we want to make here is that we have restricted this unit to the critiquing of articles. We know that students are sometimes asked to write critiques of other things: paintings, music, famous buildings, and so on. Critiques of art works require special training and special writing conventions that lie outside the scope of this book. In some fields, such as sociology, students may be asked to critique books—even as often as every two weeks. This can be particularly hard on nonnative speakers, who (understandably) may not have high reading speeds. If you find yourself in this situation, one useful strategy is to study the book reviews in the journals of your field. Such reviews should provide clues about what might be expected.

Task One

Your class has been asked to write a critique of the paper on "Patent Law Variation" by Koji Suzuki (see Task Three in Unit Five). Read this draft of the critique and answer the questions that follow.

positive — critical
balance

Critique

positive

[1]Koji Suzuki's short essay on patent law variation offers an interesting and knowledgeable discussion of an important topic. [2]The paper is, however, a little ambitious in its claims. [3]For example, Suzuki begins by claiming that "each country has its own laws . . . ," but then he seems to argue that it is only the United States that is different from everybody else. [4]Therefore, it would have been better if Suzuki had either illustrated this variation or re-

Code for criticism

stricted his discussion to the United States. [5]A second weakness, at least in my opinion, is that we are given no explanation of how and why the United States has come uniquely to adopt a first-to-invent system. [6]A sentence or two giving the historical background for this would have been helpful. [7]Even so, the final paragraph provides an excellent summary of the current situation. *positive*

1. Do you totally or partially agree with the comments in this critique? Explain your opinion.

2. Which of the sentences are complimentary and which are critical? What does this tell you about the organization of this critique? *7   phrased   2 – 5*

3. The critique contains three examples of qualification. One is the phrase "a *little* ambitious" in sentence 2. Can you find the other two? *seems to argue   at least in my opinion*

   What are the purposes of the qualifications? Could any of them be omitted? *a way to be polite, protect you from criticism   author didn't really do this*

4. Most of the critique is written in the simple present tense. Sentences 4 and 6 are not. Why do you suppose this is? *present a possibility, an alternative   suggest*

5. Sentence 5 begins with "A second weakness . . ." This is grammatically correct, although "The second weakness . . ." would be more common. Do you see any difference in meaning between the two? *no other, the only one   there are other alternatives*

Requirements for Writing Critiques

By this stage in the course, you should be quite well prepared to write critiques.

100% You have been practicing analytic reading.
You have had experience in writing an opening summary.
80% You are familiar with the role and place of qualifications or "hedges." *saying only what you can confidently say!*
0%

You have a growing sense of your instructor as audience. You are learning to present yourself in your writing as a junior member of your chosen discipline.

positioning yourself

On the other hand, for writing a successful critique, there are at least two further elements that will probably be needed: unreal conditionals and evaluative language.

In a critique, you will need to express criticism by saying what the author should have done but did not do. Two examples of this were present in Task One in sentences 4 and 6, each of which contain an unreal conditional.

4. Therefore, it *would have been* better *if* Suzuki *had* either *illustrated* this variation, or *restricted* his discussion to the United States.
6. A sentence or two giving the historical background for this *would have been* helpful.

Language Focus: Unreal Conditionals

Here are two additional examples of unreal conditional statements.

This article *would have been* more convincing *if* the author *had related* his findings to previous work on the topic.
It *would have been* better *if* the authors *had given* their main findings in the form of a table.

Notice the structure of these conditionals.

would/might have + verb-$_{EN}$ + comparison + *if* + noun phrase + *had* verb-$_{EN}$[*]

These conditionals refer to an unreal situation in the past. Note that the past perfect is used to help establish the time frame. Past unreal conditionals are common in critiques because the texts being critiqued have already been put into final form: either published or

---

[*]EN is a convention used to refer to the past participle form of the verb, e.g., write, wrote (simple past-$_{ED}$), written (participle-$_{EN}$).

turned in. There is no opportunity to revise the text in light of the criticism, because the time frame is closed. Since these conditionals express something that is impossible, linguists and philosophers often call them *counterfactuals*. In a critique, the *if*-clause in the past unreal conditional often occurs second. Why is this so?

Present unreal conditionals, on the other hand, describe a hypothetical situation in the present. In these, the past tense forms are used. In a consultation with your writing instructor, you may have heard a sentence such as this.

Your paper *would be* stronger if you *included* some additional information.

In this sentence, it is clear that the possibility for revision still exists. The time frame is open. This type of sentence is sometimes called a *hypothetical conditional.*

Task Two

Complete and exchange these thoughts with a partner.

1. My English test score would have been better if . . .
   What about you?

2. My meeting with my advisor would have gone better if . . .
   What about you?

3. My last assignment would have been better if . . .
   What about you?

Now notice the italicized verb forms in the following:

The author *should have provided* more data about her sample.
Although this is an interesting and important paper, the authors *could have given* more attention to the fact that their model of consumer choice is based entirely on U.S. data.

Notice that *should* expresses a strongly [↗ stronger] negative comment, while *could* is less strong. *Should have* is a criticism, *could have* is more a suggestion, and *might have* is a weak suggestion. [↳ weaker]

usu. = +"
to illustrate: neutral, to make st visual, give evidence
to portray: highly positive or higly negitive
136 / Academic Writing for Graduate Students

Language Focus: Evaluative Language

The final requirement for critiques is that they show appropriate use of evaluative language. All the content parts of speech can be used for this.

Nouns	success	failure
Verbs	succeed	fail
Adjectives	successful	unsuccessful
Adverbs	successfully	unsuccessfully

Evaluative Adjectives

It is typical in critiques to summarize your views by describing the source with one or two evaluative adjectives. Any of the adjectives listed in Task Three could, for example, be placed at the beginning of a closing evaluation paragraph.

In this _____ study, Jones and Wang . . .

Task Three

Rate the adjectives as follows:

+ + = very positive
+   = positive
o   = neutral, uncertain, or ambiguous
−   = negative
− − = very negative (could be fact)

(handwritten: In critique, usu. refers to you want to do a lot but you didn't make it to the amount)

unusual	limited	ambitious	modest *(a modest cost / small / small positive than small)*
small	restricted	important	flawed *(defact / small)*
useful	significant	innovative	interesting
careful	competent	impressive	elegant
simple	traditional	complex	small scale
exploratory	remarkable	preliminary *(polite negitive)*	unsatisfactory

Sometimes, we can make contrasting pairs of adjectives.

(handwritten: flawed: defact, there're st wrong, errors)
(handwritten: complex can mean complicated ↓ always negitive)

In this ambitious but flawed study, Jones and Wang . . .

innovative   preliminary
significant   limited

Can you create three other suitable combinations?

Evaluative Adjectives across the Disciplines

Classes composed of students from several disciplines do not always agree about these adjectives. This is fully understandable. Take the case of the *simple/complex* contrast. Students in science and medicine, for example, think of *simple* as a positive and *complex* as a negative. For such students *simple* equals "well-planned" or "clearly designed," and *complex* equals "confused" or "messy." In contrast, social scientists equate *simple* with "unsophisticated" and *complex* with "sophisticated."

In an interesting study (note the evaluative adjective!), Becher (1987) surveyed adjectives of praise and blame among historians, sociologists, and physicists in Britain and the United States. He found considerable differences among the three groups. Although the preferences listed in table 15 only indicate general tendencies, they are quite revealing. List some typical evaluative adjectives (both good and bad) used in your field. What about "neat" for example?

TABLE 15.   Adjectives of Praise and Blame among Historians, Sociologists, and Physicists in Britain and the United States

	Good work	Average work	Poor work
Humanities	scholarly or original	sound	thin
Social science	perceptive or rigorous	scholarly	anecdotal
Physics	elegant or economical	accurate	sloppy

Critical Reading

We will now critically read a very short report from a field that everybody in the class has at least some familiarity with: English as a Second Language. The brief research report is taken from the 1984 volume of *TESOL Quarterly*. TESOL stands for the Teachers of English to Speakers of Other Languages.

BRIEF REPORTS AND SUMMARIES

The *TESOL Quarterly* invites readers to submit short reports and updates on their work. These summaries may address any areas of interest to *Quarterly* readers. Authors' addresses are printed with these reports to enable interested readers to contact the authors for more details.

Edited by ANN FATHMAN
Cañada College

ESL Spelling Errors

LEE S. TESDELL
University of Petroleum and Minerals

■ This study investigated spelling errors in compositions written by students from four different language backgrounds at Iowa State University. Fifty-six writing samples were collected: nine from Arabic speakers, ten from Chinese speakers, twenty from Malay speakers, and seventeen from Spanish speakers. All of the students had scored 80-89 (inclusive) on the *Michigan Test of English Language Proficiency* and all had achieved a minimum of 500 on the TOEFL. They were all enrolled in academic programs at Iowa State during the 1981-1982 school year. Introductio◼

Four hypotheses were tested: 1) that ESL students at this proficiency level would make more spelling errors than native speakers, 2) that the ESL students would make more habitual errors (real mistakes) than slips (misspellings which are corrected elsewhere in the same composition), 3) that at this proficiency level there would be more spelling errors among the speakers of languages that use the Roman alphabet (Spanish, Malay) than among the speakers of languages that do not (Arabic, Chinese), and 4) that ESL students would err more frequently in the medial position of the word than initially or finally. Methods

The results showed that for the four language groups the error percentage mean was 1.88% of total words written; native speakers exhibit a 1.1% error rate (Chedru and Gerschwind, as cited in Wing and Baddeley 1980). Second, the research showed that the "slip" mean for all languages was .19 errors, while the habitual error mean was 3.66 errors. Third, contrary to Oller and Ziahosseiny's findings (1970), the difference between the non-Roman and the Roman alphabet language error percentages was found to be insignificant. Fourth, it was found that the means for error position of all four groups were as follows: initial was .428 errors, medial was 2.61 errors, and final was .66 errors. Results

The results of this study suggest that we have no evidence that spelling pedagogy should vary from language group to language group. The ESL students made more "real mistakes" than slips, which indicates that the Discussio◼

spelling skills of ESL students of all language backgrounds need to be improved. Further studies of spelling errors of other language groups and proficiency levels would help the classroom teacher of ESL to understand more about how to confront spelling problems.

REFERENCES

Chedru, F., and N. Gerschwind. 1972. Writing disturbances in acute confusional states. *Neuropsychologia* 10:343-353.

Oller, John W., and Seid M. Ziahosseiny. 1970. The constrastive analysis hypothesis and spelling errors. *Language Learning* 20(2):183-189.

Wing, Alan M., and Alan D. Baddeley. 1980. Spelling errors in handwriting. In *Cognitive processes in spelling*, Uta Frith (Ed.), 251-286. London: Academic Press.

Task Four

Read the report fairly quickly to get an idea of what it is about. Answer the following questions with a partner or in a small group.

1. The brief report is divided into four paragraphs, which we label in order, Introduction, Methods, Results, and Discussion. Does your analysis agree with these labels? If not, what labels do you suggest?

2. Why is the next to last sentence in paragraph 1 in the past perfect?

3. Notice that paragraph 2 consists of one single sentence. Look back at Unit One, figure 2, on punctuation. Can you make a suggestion for revision?

4. In paragraph 3, what evidence do you have (either for or against) that Tesdell has read Chedru and Gerschwind?

As you were reading, you probably thought of comments you would like to make about the Tesdell mini-article. Before we critique the report, we need to be *fair* to Tesdell. First, notice the comment that concludes the introduction to Brief Reports and Summaries: "Authors' addresses are printed with these reports to enable interested readers to contact the authors for more details." It is clear, we think, that Tesdell cannot be expected in such a short space to provide all the background information readers might require. In fact, Tesdell published his full report in the June 1987 issue of *Guide-*

lines. Second, we might also remember that research in ESL is not as abundant as in many other areas and may not be so sophisticated. And third, we should note that the publication date is 1984.

Task Five

Here are some criticisms of Tesdell's report made by our own classes. (Our students also had some positive comments.) Discuss the list and mark each criticism as *R*(reasonable) or *U*(unreasonable).

1. Iowa State University may not be a typical institution; therefore, the research should have been carried out across a range of universities.
2. Fifty-six writing samples is too small, especially when we remember that students are drawn from four different language backgrounds.
3. There should be equal numbers in each subgroup.
4. It is important to know more about the academic programs in which the students were enrolled, as this may affect the results.
5. In the second hypothesis, the criterion for distinguishing "slips" and "habitual errors" will not work well if the writing samples are short. In short samples, there will be little opportunity for words to be used more than once.
6. Given the sample size, the difference between 1.88% and 1.1% is unlikely to be statistically significant.

Do you have any other criticisms of Tesdell's report that you consider fair and reasonable? Work in a group to come up with at least two more. Be prepared to offer them to the class.

Task Six

Now consider the final section of this critique by one of our students. (The summary part is not given.) Which of her criticisms do you accept as being "fair and reasonable" and which "unfair and unreasonable"? What graduate program do you think Jo-Ching is in?

This study cannot prove that the hypotheses are true. The reasons are as follows:

1. The total sample size is too small, especially when it is divided into four different language backgrounds—Arabic, Chinese, Malay, and Spanish. These four groups do not represent the entire ESL population; therefore, the confidence interval needs to be reduced.

2. The investigation does not provide enough information about the population. For example, academic field, age, or amount of experience of sampled students would affect the testing outcome. In addition, if the population is non-normal, the form of the distribution will be incorrect.

3. The level of significance and the values for which the null hypothesis should be rejected in favor of alternative hypotheses are unknown; thus, the acceptable region cannot be determined.

(Jo-Ching Chen, minor editing)

Writing Critiques

So far the evaluation of Tesdell's report has been entirely negative. Negative criticism will indeed demonstrate that:

1. You understand that graduate students in the United States (and elsewhere) are expected and encouraged to criticize published work;
2. You are capable of finding points to criticize; and
3. You are beginning to express your points effectively.

However, only thinking negatively is probably ill-advised. After all, instructors rarely choose articles for critiquing because they think they are worthless. Further, you do not want to give the impression that you are only a "hatchet" person, someone who does nothing but criticize. It would be possible to structure the evaluation of the Tesdell report in this way:

Tesdell	provides	a small	piece of	interesting	topic.
	offers	minor	research	relevant	
		preliminary	on a(n)	important	

However, the study   suffers from a number of limitations.
                       exhibits several weaknesses.
                       can be criticized on several counts.
                       raises as many questions as it answers.

Finally, we should again remember the comment introducing Brief Reports and Summaries suggesting that readers can contact the author for more details. Perhaps to be fair to Tesdell, we should qualify some of our conclusions (see Unit Four). Here is an example:

> However, *at least in its published form*, the study *apparently* suffers from a number of limitations.

Task Seven

Now write your own critique of Tesdell's short paper.

Another Brief Report from *TESOL Quarterly* follows. It is a summary of an M.A. thesis written by a student from the People's Republic of China. The author, Huang, contrasts what he calls "formal" and "functional" learning strategies.

BRIEF REPORTS AND SUMMARIES

The *TESOL Quarterly* invites readers to submit short reports and updates on their work. These summaries may address any areas of interest to *Quarterly* readers. Authors' addresses are printed with these reports to enable interested readers to contact the authors for more details.

Edited by ANN FATHMAN
    College of Notre Dame

Chinese EFL Students' Learning Strategies for Oral Communication

HUANG XIAO-HUA
Guangzhou Foreign Language Institute
People's Republic of China

red introduction 5 times

■ An investigation of the learning strategies employed by Chinese EFL students for oral communication was conducted. The study attempted to identify the general strategies and specific techniques used by Chinese learners of English to improve their oral proficiency and to assess the effects of some of these. In addition, the study explored learner characteristics which are believed to affect learning strategies and techniques.

A three-part questionnaire was administered to 60 graduating English majors at Guangzhou Foreign Language Institute. Subjects were asked to specify and describe personal foreign language learning strategies (adapted from Reiss 1981); to respond to 22 items (derived from Rubin 1975 and Stern 1975) relating to their use of learning strategies and techniques; and to respond to three language learning situations. Each of the subjects also had an oral interview; this interview, modeled on the Test of Oral Interaction (a part of the *Communicative Use of English as a Foreign Language* examination series developed by the Royal Society of Arts Examination Board), was designed to evaluate ability in open-ended communicative tasks. To obtain more detailed information about the learners—in particular, their personal insights about their learning processes and strategies—the questionnaire was supplemented by interviews with the ten highest and nine lowest achievers on the oral interview.

The investigation identified a large number of learning strategies and techniques of a functional or formal nature, such as talking to oneself and memorizing lists of words. Statistical analyses (including t-tests, simple and multiple regression, and intercorrelations) demonstrated that certain strategies and techniques are critical for improvement in oral proficiency. Particularly prominent were functional strategies such as thinking in English; speaking English with other students, with teachers, and with native speakers, when available; participating actively in group oral communication activities; and reading extensively out of class. These findings confirm recommendations made by several studies (Rubin 1975, Stern 1975, Naiman, Fröhlich, Stern, and Todesco 1978) of the learning strategies of good language learners. The findings also indicate that good learners, especially those at intermediate and advanced stages, exhibit a high level of independence and that motivation plays a very important role. In addition, the findings show that good language learners in China are in many respects similar to good language learners elsewhere.

The interviews revealed a number of interesting similarities and differences in language learning behavior. While good language learners did not all use the same techniques, those they used were all functional in nature and directed at meaning. Also, while these learners were all highly motivated, the reasons for their motivation to learn English varied, as did their language learning histories. For the poorer learners, the cause of low motivation was generally the same—for example, failure to pass the examinations for science majors, followed by a change to an English major—but the learning techniques they used differed considerably. One student reported trying to use strategies employed by a good language learner and finding them unsuitable. This and other findings suggest the complexity and sometimes idiosyncratic character of foreign language learning processes. (M.A. Thesis, The Chinese University of Hong Kong, 1984)

REFERENCES

Naiman, Neil, Maria Fröhlich, H.H. Stern, and Angela Todesco. 1978. *The good language learner*. Research in Education Series 7. Toronto: Ontario Institute for Studies in Education.

Reiss, Mary-Ann. 1981. Helping the unsuccessful language learner. *The Modern Language Journal* 65(2):121-128.

Rubin, Joan. 1975. What the "good language learner" can teach us. *TESOL Quarterly* 9(1):41-51.

Stern, H.H. 1975. What can we learn from the good language learner? *Canadian Modern Language Review* 31(4):304-318.

Task Eight

Study Huang's report, then list examples of functional learning strategies.

Functional Strategies

1. _talking to aesat_
2. _memory a lot of words_
3. Speaking English with others
4. _thinking in English_
5. _reading extensively out of class_

Language Focus: Inversions

You already know that English usually requires an inverted word order for questions. You also probably know that a different word order is required if a "negative" word is used to open a sentence.

not only... but also

Not only has the author presented some valuable new information, he has also presented it in a very clear and coherent manner.
In no case do the authors provide any statistical information about their results.

Notice how the auxiliary verb precedes the subject, as in a question. Now look at this statement, first inverted, then in normal word order.

(*One time in a paper*)

Particularly prominent were functional strategies . . .
Functional strategies . . . were particularly prominent.

This kind of inversion, even with simple adjectives or participles, is quite common in poetry ("Broken was the sword of the king"). However, in academic English, it only occurs with emphatic ("particularly") or comparative ("even more") expressions. The inversion is a strong highlighting device and should only be used for special emphasis, as when we want to single out *one* result/fault/problem/ virtue from many others. Six typical expressions follow. Complete three of the five that have not been done for you.

1. Particularly important + BE + Noun Phrase . . .
      was the discovery that many computer viruses have no known source.
2. Especially interesting _____
3. Much less expected _____
4. Rather more significant _____
5. Especially noteworthy _____
6. Of greater concern _____

Task Nine

Now write a critique of a paper from your own field or a critique of the Brief Report by Huang.

If you choose Huang, notice that the four paragraphs provide, in order, Introduction, Methods, Results, and Discussion. Look through each carefully and note what you consider to be the strengths and weaknesses of each section. In addition, you may wish to consider whether you agree with the following more general points:

1. Given the space constraints, Huang nicely integrates previous research in this area.
2. At the close of the results paragraph, Huang notes that good language learners in China are similar to those elsewhere. This finding is interesting and surprising, since many people seem to think that Chinese learners are somewhat different.
3. The last sentence underlines the fact that Huang is research- ing a complex topic. (In comparison to Tesdell?)

The final major text in this unit is also taken from *TESOL Quar- terly's* Brief Reports and Summaries. However, we offer it here in a slightly adapted form. For our purposes, we will consider it a draft manuscript. For the moment, just read it quickly to get an idea of what it is about.

Rhetorical Patterns in English and Japanese
Hiroe Kobayashi

A study was conducted to investigate differences in U.S. and Japanese students' use of rhetorical patterns in their first language writing and Japanese students' use of their first language patterns in English writing.

A total of 678 writing samples was obtained from 226 students representing four groups: U.S. college students (AEA), Japanese advanced ESL students in the U.S. (JEA), and two groups of college students in Japan—English majors (JEJ) and non-English majors (JJJ). The two groups in the U.S. and the JEJ group wrote in English, while the JJJ group wrote in Japanese. Each student was asked to write three compositions—two semi-controlled compositions based on pictures and one free composition on an assigned topic—involving narrative and expository modes.

The writing samples were examined for the placement of a general statement. Each of the samples was coded by native speakers of the two languages as exemplifying one of four rhetorical patterns: (1) General-to-Specific (GS), (2) Specific-to-General (SG), (3) General Statement in the middle (MG), and (4) Omission of a General Statement (OM).

The study found that the four groups differed from each other in their use of these patterns. U.S. students (AEA) frequently chose the GS pattern; that is, they wrote a general statement first and followed it with specifics. Japanese students writing in Japanese (JJJ) frequently chose the SG pattern; they began with specifics that led to a general statement. The two Japanese groups writing in English showed clearly different tendencies; the JEA group fell between the two culturally different groups writing in their first language (JJJ and AEA), while the JEJ group reflected very closely the preferences of the JJJ group. The JEJ and JJJ groups also chose the OM pattern more frequently than the two groups in America.

Although these findings indicate that the differences among

the four groups are not absolute but rather a matter of degree, they do suggest (1) the existence of cultural preferences for certain rhetorical patterns, and (2) a tendency for Japanese ESL learners to use first language patterns when writing in English.
(Adapted from *TESOL Quarterly* 18 (1984): 737–38)

Language Focus: Special Verb Agreements

Notice the agreement of the first subject and verb in the second paragraph of Kobayashi's report.

A total of 678 writing samples was obtained . . .

This sentence follows the standard rule whereby the verb agrees with the subject noun (in this case *total*) and not the second noun (in this case *samples*). But now note that this important rule does not apply in a few exceptional cases, such as when the first noun is a fraction, a proportion, or a percentage. In these special cases, the verb agrees with the noun *closest* to the verb.

A minority of the students *were* native speakers.

Fill in the blank with either *was* or *were*.

1. The average score of all the results ___was___ 67.8%.

2. A total of 7,000 students ___was___ required to take the test.

3. Half of the students ___were___ asked to answer an experimental question.

4. Nearly 19% of the candidates ___were___ unable to complete the test within the time limit.

5. Approximately 46% of the test population ___was___ *were* from overseas.

6. One quarter of the students _____*were*_____ required to take the test again.

Another interesting grammar point arises in sentences beginning with *a . . . number of/the . . . number of*. Which form of *be* would you choose here?

A small number of African students _____*were*_____ included on an experimental basis.

The small number of Japanese candidates _____ thought to be surprising.

Reaction Papers

Throughout this book, we have placed strong emphasis on formal style. We will continue to do so in Units Seven and Eight. However, in this section of Unit Six we would like to introduce you to two kinds of critique that permit—and encourage—a more personal and informal style of writing: reaction papers and reviews.

In a reaction paper, students are encouraged to draw on their own experiences, feelings, and ideas as well as to make methodological and analytic comments. International students often have an advantage here because they can incorporate observations and experiences that reflect their own special backgrounds. Often these comments will open instructors' eyes to things they had not thought of.

Task Ten

Here is part of a reaction paper on the Kobayashi report written by a Japanese student. Since the student is Japanese, she can be expected, of course, to have her own personal "angle" on Kobayashi's conclusions. Read what she has written and answer the questions that follow.

[1]It is my opinion that Dr. Kobayashi has carried out a useful piece of research. [2]Her findings should help American English teachers to understand the problems we Japanese have in writing English.

³However, I am not sure that her interpretation of the results is correct. ⁴She claims that her findings "suggest the existence of cultural preferences for certain rhetorical patterns." ⁵I think Americans are taught in high school to begin their compositions with a general statement, while in Japan we are taught differently. ⁶Is this "culture"? ⁷I think it may be a difference in education system.

1. Make a list of all the personal expressions used in this reaction paper.

2. Which sentences are positive, which negative, and which neutral? What does this tell us about the way the text is organized?

3. In which sentence does the author make effective use of her own experience?

4. Sentence 6 is a direct question. In our experience, using direct questions is very popular among Asian students. Why do you think they do this? And can you find an alternative way of concluding by joining the last two sentences together?

Language Focus: Scare Quotes (use it in paper!)

Earlier in Unit Six, we mentioned word inversion as a result of putting "negative" words at the beginning of sentences. The word *negative* in the previous sentence is in "scare quotes." The use of scare quotes is a means of distancing the writer from the descriptor. The writer indicates by scare quotes that she or he does not necessarily believe that the concept is valid. For instance, the use of quotes around *negative* in our example, suggests that negative is to be interpreted very broadly, since it will cover words like *hardly* and *scarcely* as well as "true" negatives (note the scare quotes!) such as *never*.

In critiques, scare quotes are a useful way to signal that you are not necessarily committed to the author's position. For example, you might write:

" CJones, 1997, p.) → stress

According to Jones, Halloween is a silly holiday. → stress

(Italic)

⸗ ____" underline → informal

Kobayashi's conclusions about "cultural" preferences . . .

The scare quotes indicate that you have doubts about the validity of Kobayashi's position. Scare quotes are a useful demonstration of your sophistication. However, they tend to be used more in social sciences and humanities than in science and engineering.

Task Eleven

Now write a reaction paragraph to one of the three main texts introduced in this unit (by Tesdell, Huang, and Kobayashi) or to a paper from your own field. If you choose a paper from your own field, you may want to comment on why a particular methodology may or may not be useful for your own research.

As it happens, an increasing number of journals are now printing readers' "reactions," "responses," or "discussions" to published articles. Do you know of such a journal in your field? If you can find such a journal, you will see the large difference in style between the research article and the commentary.

Reviews

We now turn to manuscript critiques by journal reviewers. Below is a review of the Kobayashi manuscript by an external reviewer, which was requested by the editor. Imagine you have been appointed as a graduate student editorial assistant to the editor of the *TESOL Quarterly*, Professor Ann Jones. The editor has asked you to evaluate the manuscript and the review.

Task Twelve

What do you think of comments 1 through 7 below? Place your judgment in the blank provided.

+ + = strongly agree with the reviewer
+   = generally agree, but maybe not too important
?   = unsure
−   = disagree but no big deal
− − = strongly disagree

Professor Ann Jones
Editor, *TESOL Quarterly*
Central State University
Midwest, MW 36901

Dear Ann,

Thank you for giving me the opportunity to review the Kobayashi manuscript submitted to the Brief Reports section. My general conclusion is that it is basically acceptable for publication in *TESOL Quarterly*. I list my comments and observations below.

___ 1. The sample size and its binational origin is impressively large. K is to be congratulated on the quantitative dimensions of the research.

___ 2. That said, it seems unfortunate that she (or is it he?) was unable to find a group of American students trying to write in Japanese. This would have better balanced the groups, but I know it is probably difficult to find large numbers of such students. Overall I do not think that this imbalance affects the publishability of the report.

___ 3. K gives the impression that the coders never had any disagreements or found any compositions that did not fit into the four-way scheme. I am not sure whether a brief report need deal with such details, but I mention it in passing.

___ 4. Personally, I find the group abbreviations (JJJ, etc.) somewhat confusing. I do not have a solution. Perhaps you can think of one?

___ 5. In the results paragraph, K says that one group "frequently" chose one pattern, and another group another. What does "frequently" mean here? Is it 60–75–90% of the time? Even in a brief report, I think readers would expect some numbers here.

___ 6. The final paragraph makes some claims. The second is obviously true (and rather obvious). The first is rather bold. The evidence for different rhetorical patterns is based on student writing rather than published writing. We may be looking at teacher instructions and expectations rather than genuine cultural differences. As a result, I think the conclusion could be modified or qualified in some way.

___ 7. Following up on my previous point, I think the title is much too broad.

Thank you again for asking me to review this interesting report. I would welcome further opportunities of this kind,

Sincerely,

Dennis Lum

Compare your judgments with a fellow student (who also happens to be an editorial assistant). Try and resolve any differences. If you and your partner have strong disagreements with the reviewer, explain your position to your instructor (as if he or she were the editor).

Task Thirteen

On the basis of your judgments and your discussions, write a letter to Hiroe Kobayashi accepting the report (in principle) but suggesting a number of changes. Write to Dr. Kobayashi (who is a woman) on behalf of Dr. Jones and yourself. Neither of you know Dr. Kobayashi, and this is an official letter. Use *we* but write the letter in a fairly formal style.

A Final Look at the ESL Literature

We have now reached the end of the work on critiques. In Units Seven and Eight, you will review the previous literature as part of writing a research paper. Now we ask you only to *respond* to attempts at summarizing the three papers by Tesdell, Huang, and Kobayashi while they are still fresh in your minds.

Task Fourteen

Below are four versions of an overview of the literature. As you read them, you may notice that they vary in a number of ways. Complete table 16, which follows the texts.

Version A

The readings provide conflicting evidence as to whether ESL students from different language backgrounds vary in performance and behavior. Kobayashi (1984) reports differences in writing rhetorical patterns. Huang (1985) concludes that good language learners in the People's Republic of China follow strategies adopted by good language learners elsewhere. Oller et al. (1970), as cited by Tesdell, found that spelling errors varied according to the L1 writing system, but Tesdell (1984) found no such variation.

Version B

From a scientific perspective, recent studies aimed at investigating whether language and cultural background influence the learning of English are unsatisfactory. The available work (1–3) is small-scale and reported only in summary form. Weaknesses in experimental design and inadequacies in statistical tests mean that no conclusions can be drawn at the present time. Further research is necessary.

Version C

There are at least four papers relevant to the question of background variation in ESL. The earliest found that the L1 writing system had an effect on spelling errors (Oller et al. 1970), but later work contradicts this finding (Tesdell 1984). Japanese may be influenced by their background in the way they organize their writing in English (Kobayashi 1984). On the other hand, good language learners may be similar all over the world (Huang 1985).

Version D

Tesdell (1984) found that spelling did not vary according to language group, although he cites an earlier study (Oller et al. 1970) showing variation according to Roman/non-Roman writing systems. Specific rhetorical patterns in writing were identified for

Japanese speakers by Kobayashi (1984). In apparent contrast, Huang (1985) seemed to show that at least good language learners in the People's Republic of China adopted similar strategies to those identified elsewhere (e.g., Rubin 1975). It is difficult to draw conclusions from these findings, except perhaps to speculate that background may affect performance but not learning style.

What are your preferences regarding these issues in table 16? And what are the preferences of your field?

TABLE 16.   Analysis Chart

	A	B	C	D
Is the version general-specific (SG) or specific-general (SG)	GS	SG		
Is the main tense past or present?				
Are the citations by name or number?				
When citing by name, do the names occur (a) as subject, (b) as agent, or (c) in parentheses?				
Is the version a summary or a critique?				

(In spite of) X's description / claims that A + B are not necessarily completely different / mutually exclusive, however, Y + Z argue that M + N.---, entirely distinct

The authors presented a new approach to understand the expansion of mass schooling claiming that it has taken place universally.   an -ing clause of result

Unit Seven
Constructing a Research Paper I

Units Seven and Eight consolidate many of the aspects of academic writing that we have stressed in earlier units. However, they also break new ground. They differ from the previous units in one important way. By this stage, we think it possible that you may now be carrying out a research investigation of some kind. The purpose of these units, therefore, is to prepare you for and help you with writing up your own research. In order to do this, we have made two further assumptions:

You will be using a typical organizational pattern for your
  paper—in other words, the IMRD format (Introduction,
  Methods, Results, and Discussion) or some variant of it;
You hope that your paper might be published.

So, where do we stand? As we can see from the following list, we have already made good progress toward carrying out the difficult task of writing a research paper.

Parts of the Research Paper	Contributions so far
Title	
Abstract	Unit Five, Summary Writing
Introduction	Unit Two, General-specific
	Unit Four, Problem-solution
	Unit Six, Critiques
Methods	Unit Three, Process descriptions
Results	Unit Four, Highlight statements
	Unit Four, Qualifications
Discussion	Unit Four, Explanations (of unexpected results, etc.)
	Unit Six, Literature comparisons
Acknowledgments	
References	

155

We can also see from the list that there is some more work to be done. The really difficult areas, especially Introductions and Discussions, need considerable attention. We also need to consider writing up Methods and Results for research papers (RPs), as opposed to, say, lab reports. There are some smaller bits of business, such as acknowledgments and titles to be discussed. Even so, enough has been done to make it possible.

When you read an RP, you may *think* that it is a simple, straightforward account of an investigation—indeed, RPs are often designed to create this impression. However, we believe that such impressions are largely misleading. Writers of RPs, in our opinion, operate in a *strategic* manner. This is principally because such writers know that RPs have to justify themselves. They need to establish that the research questions are sufficiently interesting. They need to demonstrate that the research questions are, in theory, answerable. And they need to compete against other RPs for acceptance and recognition. As a result, RP authors are very much concerned with *positioning*—with showing that their studies are relevant and significant and have some new contribution to make.

Overview of the Research Paper

The overall rhetorical shape of a typical RP is shown in figure 10.

This diagram gives a useful indication of the out-in-out or general-specific-general movement of the typical RP. As the RP in English has developed over the last hundred years or so, the four different sections have thus become identified with four different purposes.

Introduction (I)   The main purpose of the Introduction is to provide the rationale for the paper, moving from general discussion of the topic to the particular question or hypothesis being investigated. A secondary purpose is to attract interest in the topic—and hence readers.

Methods (M)   The Methods section describes, in various degrees of detail, methodology, materials, and procedures. This is the narrowest part of the RP.

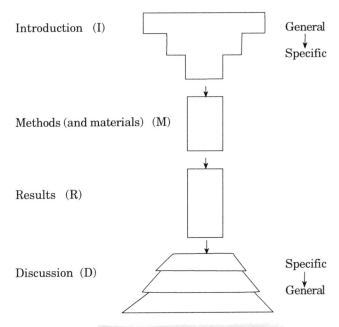

Fig. 10. Overall shape of a research paper

Results (R)	In the Results section, the findings are described, accompanied by variable amounts of commentary.
Discussion (D)	The Discussion section offers an *increasingly generalized* account of what has been learned in the study. This is usually done through a series of "points," at least some of which refer back to statements made in the Introduction.

As a result of these different purposes, the four sections have taken on different linguistic characteristics. We summarize some of these in table 17. The first line of the table shows, for instance, that the present tense is common in Introductions and Discussions, but uncommon in Methods and Results.

Task One

In 1993 Dorothea Thompson published a useful RP on Results sections in biochemistry articles. She was particularly interested in

TABLE 17. Frequencies of Selected Items in RP Sections

	Introduction	Methods	Results	Discussion
Present tense	high	low	low	high
Past tense	mid	high	high	mid
Passive voice	low	high	variable	variable
Citations/references	high	low	variable	high
Qualification	mid	low	mid	high
Commentary	high	low	variable	high

what kinds of comments researchers made in their Results sections and whether researchers followed the guidelines in manuals. Here are eight sentences from her paper. Based on table 17 and on your own knowledge, can you guess from which of the sections they come? Mark each one *I*, *M*, *R*, or *D*. There are two sentences from each section. Work with a partner, if possible.

D 1. Only further research can determine the applicability of this study's findings to scientific disciplines outside biochemistry.

M 2. The data were analyzed both qualitatively and quantitatively.

M 3. Short communications and mini-reviews were excluded from the sample because these publications have different objectives and use a different format from that of the experimental research article.

I 4. The assumptions underlying this study are grounded largely in sociological accounts of the scientific enterprise (Knorr-Cetina, 1981; Latour, 1987; Latour and Woolgar, 1979).

D 5. These style guides are, at best, superficial descriptions of the content of these sections.

R 6. In 15 of the sample articles, these methodological narratives included explicit justifications for the selection of certain technical procedures, laboratory equipment, or alternatives to standard protocols.

D 7. Scientific style manuals reinforce the conception that Results sections simply present experimental data in a

LR

"cold," purely objective, expository manner (Council of Biology Editors, 1972; Day, 1988; Mitchell, 1968; Woodford, 1968).

8. In 38% of the JBC Results sections sampled, Kornberg and his co-authors directly relate their findings to those of earlier studies, as the following illustrate: . . .

I.

LR

Methods

You might have expected us to begin our discussion of RP sections with the Introduction. Instead, we are beginning with Methods. This is usually the easiest section to write and, in fact, it is often the section that researchers write first.

In Units Seven and Eight, we will involve you in the writing up of a very small research investigation of our own. Among other things, we hope in this way to illustrate certain strategic aspects of RP writing. We summarize our miniproject in Task Two.

You will remember from Unit One that sentence connectors are words like *however* and *therefore*. We became interested in the *position* of sentence connectors in written academic English sentences. We became curious about this since we found that the standard grammars of English had little to say on this topic. We are currently writing up our small-scale investigation. Like many other academics, we started with Methods.

Task Two

Here is our draft. Please read it and answer the questions that follow.

Methods

[1]In order to investigate the position of connectors, we examined their occurrence in academic papers published in three journals. [2]The sample consisted of all the main articles appearing in the third issues of the 1992 volumes of *College Composition and Communication, English for Specific Purposes*, and *Research in the Teaching of English*. [3](See Appendix A for a list of the articles

studied.) [4]The sample amounted to about 230 running pages of text, comprising 12 articles (four from each journal). [5]Each occurrence of a connector was identified, highlighted, and then coded for one of three positions in a clause. [6]If the connector was the first or last word in the clause, it was designated "initial" or "final" respectively. [7]If it occurred in any other position, it was classified as "medial." [8]The following examples illustrate the coding system:

A t-test was run;

however, the results were insignificant.	Initial
the results, *however*, were insignificant.	Medial
the results were, *however*, insignificant.	Medial
the results were insignificant, *however*.	Final

[9]For the purposes of this study, the category of sentence connector was interpreted quite broadly. [10]We included items like *unfortunately* that are sometimes considered to be sentence adverbs. [11]We included such items as *as it were* and *in turn*, which have an uncertain grammatical status. [12]We also counted conjunctions like *but* as connectors when they occurred as *first* elements in sentences, because they seemed to be functioning as connectors in these contexts.

1. As is customary, the main tense in our Methods section is the past. In one sentence, however, the main verb is in the present. Which one is it and why?

2. Consider the following subject-verb combinations from sentences in our Methods section:

   1. we examined . . .
   5. each occurrence was identified . . .
   6. it was designated . . .
   7. it was classified . . .
   9. the category was interpreted . . .
   10. we included . . .
   11. we included . . .
   12. we counted . . .

These eight sentences describe what we did. As you can see, in four cases we used the past passive, and in four cases we used *we* and the past active. Is this switching acceptable to you? Could you do this in your field? What would your advisor or instructor recommend? Do you think we should have been consistent? In other words, do you think we should have used either the passive or *we* all the way through?

In a classic 1981 paper, Tarone et al. argue that the choice of passive versus *we* + active is not always a "free" stylistic choice. According to Tarone et al., the passive in the astrophysics papers they examined is used for standard procedures, while the use of *we* signals something new or unexpected. Do you think this might be true of your field?

3. Do you think the third paragraph should come before the second? What are the advantages and disadvantages of such a change?

4. As it happens, our account of Methods is not quite accurate. In actual fact, we conducted a pilot study on one journal. When that experience appeared to work out, we extended the sample. Is there any good reason for mentioning this part of the (true) story? When you write up a Methods section, is it appropriate to simplify or straighten out the actual process? Is it OK to "tidy up" in this way?

5. Finally, would you like to guess what our results were? What percentage of connectors were initial, medial, and final?

Language Focus: Imperatives in Research Papers

In the Methods section in Task Two, sentence 3 currently reads:

(See Appendix A for a list of the articles studied.)

We could, of course, have written:

(A list of the articles studied is given in Appendix A.)

Command-like imperatives are common in textbooks, manuals, lectures, and labs.

Analyze the results in figure 1.
Complete the following sentences.
Notice the relationship between A and B.
Prepare 5cc of distillate.
Carry this total *forward*.

In RPs, however, imperatives are less commonly used because they may be offensive. They may upset the fragile relationship between the writer and the reader, since the reader (instructor, advisor, or someone outside) can be expected to have a status comparable to or higher than the author.

However, one verb is widely used in many RP fields. Indeed, it may account for up to 50% of all the (occasional) uses of the imperative in research writing. As you may have guessed by now, that verb is *let*.

Let *p* stand for the price-cost ratio
Let *N* equal the number of consumers

A few other imperative verbs can be found in mathematical arguments, such as *suppose, substitute*, and *assume*.

A rather more difficult case occurs when you want to direct your readers' attention to some particular point, as we did when we wrote "(See Appendix A for a list of . . .)." We wanted the readers to know at this point in our paper that we have elsewhere provided full details of our data.

In RPs would you accept imperative uses of the following, and, if so, can you provide an example?

1. Notice
2. Consider
3. Imagine
4. Note
5. Refer
6. Compare
7. Recall

8. Observe
9. Take the case of, etc.
10. Disregard

If you think that an imperative might cause *offense* by being impolite, there are easy ways of escape.

Imperative	Now compare the results in tables 4 and 5.
Passive	The results in tables 4 and 5 can now be compared.
Conditional	If we now compare the results in tables 4 and 5, we can see that . . .

Writing Up a Methods Section

One of us (John) interviewed a student planning her first research paper for her masters in social work. Mei-Lan said that the provisional title for her research paper was "Chinese Elderly Living in the United States: A Problem-free Population?" She said that she had chosen this topic because of some "prevailing myths" that the Chinese communities would always look after their elderly and that such elderly would not accept help from outsiders. She believed that certain traditional Chinese attitudes, such as "filial piety," were beginning to change in U.S. communities. She added that all the research to date had been conducted in the large communities in big cities on the East and West Coasts. She wanted to study smaller communities in a midwest town. John then asked her about methodology.

John Swales: How are you going to collect your data?
Mei-Lan: By face-to-face interviews. I want to do one-on-one interviews because I think if other family members are there the interviewees will not reveal their deep feelings and real problems.
JS: How will you find your subjects?
ML: I'll use friends and acquaintances in the local Chinese community to introduce me.
JS: Will you record the interviews?

ML: Yes, but of course I will ask permission first.

JS: Will you use English?

ML: The interviewees can use any language they prefer—Mandarin, Taiwanese, or English. Whatever is most comfortable for them.

JS: How long do you plan the interviews to last, and do you have a fixed list of questions?

ML: About an hour. I have a list of questions but I do not want to follow them very exactly. I will use what sociologists call "semi-structured" interviews. Part planned, part "go with the flow," as the Americans say.

JS: Finally, how many people will you interview?

ML: Because of limited time and contacts, only about ten. So I will be doing a qualitative analysis. There will not be enough subjects for statistics.

Task Three

Now with a partner draft the *first* sentence of Mei-Lan's Methods section. Remember to use formal style. You may wish to consider which of the following elements should be included.

1. methodology
2. the purpose of the methodology
3. the sample

Task Four

Now write a Methods section of your own. If you do not have any suitable material, you could—as an alternative—complete Mei-Lan's Methods section for her. In this case, assume that she has now completed the work.

Methods Sections across Disciplines

The two Methods sections we have been working on so far would fall under the broad category of "social science." Studies show that most Methods sections in social science disciplines share a number of characteristics:

They are explicit about details and procedures.
They are slow paced since they do not presume much background knowledge,
They contain justifications, explanations, and (sometimes) examples.
The terminology is often repeated.

In social science, education, public health, and so on, methodology is often a very important and hotly debated issue. Indeed, in some cases in these areas, the main point of an RP will be to announce some development in method. However, in science, engineering, and medical research, standard practices and established methods are much more widely available. As a result, Methods sections in these fields may be very different.

Task Five

Read this opening to a Methods section and answer the questions that follow.

Methods for Analysis and Functional Properties

The standard AOAC[1] methods (AOAC, 1975) were used for the determination of total solids, nitrogen, crude fat, ash, and Vitamin C. Total sugars were determined by the method of Potter et al. (1968), and the total carbohydrates (in terms of glucose) were assayed according to the procedure of Dubois et al. (1956). The method of Kohler and Patten (1967) was followed for determining amino acid composition.
                          (Quoted by Knorr-Cetina 1981, 157)

1. What field do you think this extract comes from? *Science (nutrition , chemistry)*

2. What differences can you note between this Methods section and the one given in Task Two? What evidence can you find here of shared background knowledge? What is striking about the ways in which the methods in this passage are described (or, more exactly, not described)?

---

[1]AOAC = Association of Operational Analytic Chemists

3. Would a Methods section written like this be possible in your field?

Task Six

We can conclude that Methods sections vary greatly in what we might call "speed."

Type 1	Slow (as in our own draft)
Type 2	Fairly slow
Type 3	Fairly fast
Type 4	Fast (as in the paper quoted by Knorr-Cetina)

Here is part of a Methods section written by one of our students. She is working on a Ph.D. in physiology. What "speed" would you give it?

Suppose Jun's advisor suggested that it could be "speeded up" a little. What advice do you have? There are also a couple of small mistakes toward the end. Can you correct those as well?

Binding Assay and Down Regulation Study

Cells were cultured in 24-well plates. Receptor binding was determined by incubating the intact cells with (3H)NMS in 1 ml buffer A at 4°C or 37°C. Non-specific binding was defined in the presence of atropine. Incubation was terminated by washing the cells with ice-cold saline three times. Cells were scraped in 0.5ml water and suspensions were put into 5mm bio-safe scintillation fluid and then counted in a Beckman liquid scintillation counter. For the study of down regulation, cells was pre-incubated with 10mm M CCh for different periods time and then washed with a buffer A three times. The binding assay was performed as described above.

(Jun Yang, unedited)

Where on the "speed" scale (Types 1–4) would you place your own methods descriptions and those typical of your field?

Language Focus: Hyphens in Noun Phrases

Notice that Jun's first sentence ends with the noun phrase "24-well plates." <u>Hyphens are often used to clarify how complex noun phrases are to be interpreted.</u> In Jun's case, her hyphen indicated that she was using plates containing 24 wells. Without the hyphen, the phrase could be interpreted as 24 plates containing an un-specified number of wells. What differences can you see between the following pairs of noun phrases?

small-car factory / small car factory
blue-lined paper / blue lined paper
university-paid personnel / university paid personnel

Read the above pairs aloud. Can you make a distinction between them in terms of stress and intonation?

Can you think of one or two similar pairs from your own field?

How would you indicate what you meant by the following noun phrases? All three are ambiguous, at least out of context.

artificial heart valve
rapid release mechanism
strong acting director

temporary

Results

The other section we will deal with in this unit is the Results sec-tion. Again we will begin by asking you to read the Results section of our own paper. As it stands at present, it is an incomplete draft.

Results

A total of 467 sentence connectors was found, averaging just over two per page. Eleven of the 12 articles used connectors with some frequency, with totals ranging from 24 to 58. The one exception was the only article in the sample that dealt with literary texts,

You can't will numbers at the beginning. Gw. II.

which used only nine connectors. The scarcity of connectors in this paper may be due to its heavy use of commentary on literary passages.

Seventy different sentence connectors occurred in the sample. This large number is somewhat surprising, even taking into account our broad interpretation of "connector." Those that occurred four times or more are listed in decreasing frequency of use in table 18.

TABLE 18.   Frequency of Connectors

Rank	Item	Total occurrence
1	however	62
2	first, second, etc.	52
3	thus	33
4	also	30
5	for example	29
6	in addition	20
7	finally	19
8	therefore	16
9	on the other hand	14
10	then	12
11	nevertheless	11
	for instance	
	furthermore	
14	moreover	9
	in particular	
	but	
17	in fact	8
	yet	
19	that is	6
	in contrast	
	in other words	
22	further	5
	similarly	
	of course	
25	as a result	4

There are a number of surprises in the frequency data. There was unexpectedly heavy use of the "informal" connectors *but* (nine instances) and *yet* (eight instances). Although these are known to be frequent in newspapers and correspondence, we were somewhat surprised to find so many in refereed scholarly journals. In contrast, there was minimal use of "conclusives," such as *in conclusion*. Under 2% of all the connectors fell into this category. Finally, very uneven frequencies in certain other categories were noted.

Contrasts: however, 62   nevertheless, 11   all the same, 0
Results: thus, 33   therefore, 16   hence, 1

We now turn to the positional data. Of the 467 connectors found, 352 occurred in initial position (75.4%), 109 in medial position, and only six in final position. Clearly, final position is very rare in this kind of writing, and we will not discuss it further. If we now examine the positional data in terms of individual connectors, we find that different connectors behave somewhat differently. In table 19 all connectors occurring four times or more are categorized for percentage of occurrence in initial position. (Informal uses of *but* and *yet* have been excluded.)

TABLE 19.   Positional Categories of Connectors

Category	Connectors	Occurrence
A	First, second, etc., in addition, nevertheless, finally, that is, as a result	100% in initial position
B	moreover, thus, in particular/in fact, in other words, of course	Between 75% and 99% in initial position
C	however, for instance, on the other hand, furthermore	Between 50% and 74% in initial position
D	also, for example, therefore, then	Between 25% and 49% in initial position

Task Seven

Go back and read through the Results section of our paper, underlining all the occasions where we have used numbers (ignore percentages). Can you determine the rules we followed for when to write numbers as digits (12, etc.) and when as words (twelve, etc.)? What are the rules you use in your field?

Task Eight

Notice that our Results section is not complete. Suppose we asked you what we could include in the concluding paragraph to our Results Section, based on the information in table 18? What highlighting statements would you suggest? Refer back to Unit Four if necessary. Give your suggestions in order, from the first statement to be included to the last.

Commentary in Results Sections

It is often said that the Results section of an RP should simply report the data that has been collected; that is, it should focus exclusively on the present results. Indeed, many of the books and manuals aiming at helping students and scholars to write research papers offer this kind of advice. These books argue, particularly, that all evaluation and commentary should be left until the Discussion. However, research shows that this distinction between Results and Discussion is not as sharp as commonly believed. For example, Thompson (1993) studied the Results sections from 20 published biochemistry papers. Table 20 presents what she found.

This is part of Thompson's conclusions:

> My research demonstrates that scientists—in this case biochemists—do not present results only in a factual expository manner; they also employ a variety of rhetorical moves to argue for the validity of scientific facts and knowledge claims.

(P. 126)

TABLE 20. Commentary Found in Results Sections

Type of commentary	Number of papers (max. = 20)
Justifying the methodology	19
Interpreting the results	19
Citing agreement with previous studies	11
Commenting on the data	10
Admitting difficulties in interpretation	8
Pointing out discrepancies	4
Calling for further research	0

Authors often include commentary because they are aware of their audience. They can *anticipate* that their readers may be thinking, "Why did they use this method rather than that one?" or "Isn't this result rather strange?" For obvious reasons, authors may not want to postpone responding to such imaginary questions and critical comments until the final section.

Task Nine

Carefully read a Results section that you have written or read from your field and our draft on sentence connectors, marking any commentary elements. In your estimation, which of the following types are the passages most like?

Type 1   Gives straightforward description of the author's results; includes no commentary at all (no comparisons with the work of others, no justifications, no—or very few—obvious highlighting statements).

Type 2   Is mostly restricted to present findings, but includes a few minor uses of commentary.

Type 3   Consists of both description of findings and a number of commentary elements; uses several of the categories mentioned by Thompson.

Type 4   Makes heavy use of commentary; uses most of the categories found by Thompson; could almost be taken for a discussion.

Be prepared to discuss your findings in class. Bring the passage from your field with you.

Task Ten

Produce a Results section from your own work (or part of one if your work is extensive). If your results are not yet complete, create some findings on your own. Alternatively, you may complete the final paragraph of the Results section for the sentence connector mini-RP.

Unit Eight
Constructing a Research Paper II

In this final unit, we deal with the remaining parts of a research
paper in the following order:

Introduction sections
Discussion sections
Acknowledgments
Titles
Abstracts

Introduction Sections

It is widely recognized that writing introductions is slow, difficult,
and troublesome for both native speakers as well as nonnative
speakers. A very long time ago, the Greek philosopher Plato re-
marked, "The beginning is half of the whole." Indeed, eventually
producing a good Introduction section always seems like a battle
hard won.

Writing the Introduction of an RP is particularly troublesome. In
some kinds of texts, such as term papers or case reports, it is possible to start immediately with a topic or thesis statement

The purpose of this paper is to . . . *boring*
This paper describes and analyzes . . .
My aim in this paper is to . . .
In this paper, we report on . . .

However, this kind of opening is rare and unusual in an RP (probably under 10% of published RPs start in this way). In fact, statements like those above typically come at or near the end of an RP
Introduction. Why is this? And what comes before?

We believe that the answer to these questions lies in two interconnected parts. The first half of the answer lies in the need to appeal to
the readership. In a term paper assignment, the reader is set. (In-

deed the reader is *required* to read and evaluate your paper!) On the other hand, a paper that is designed for the external world—if only in theory—needs to attract an audience. We can illustrate this by taking the case of one of those few published papers that actually does start by describing the present research. Here is the opening sentence of the Introduction:

> This study of the writing of 22 first graders and 13 third graders is concerned with how children learn the rules of punctuation.
> (Cordeiro 1988, 62)

The Cordeiro paper, "Children's Punctuation: An Analysis of Errors in Period Placement," was published in a journal called *Research in the Teaching of English*. As the title of this journal indicates, the journal covers several different research areas. Doubtless, the very specific opening to the Cordeiro paper will appeal immediately to those researchers actively involved in the topic. On the other hand, it is likely at the same time to "turn off" many other readers of the journal—readers who have no interest in this precise research area.

We believe that we can best explain the second half of the answer by using a metaphor—that of *competition* as it is used in ecology. Just as plants compete for light and space, so writers of RPs compete for acceptance and recognition. In order to obtain this acceptance and recognition, most writers use an organizational pattern that contains the following three "moves" in table 21, in the order given.

Creating a Research Space

In summary, then, the Introduction sections of RPs typically follow the pattern in table 21 in response to two kinds of competition: competition for research space and competition for readers. We can call this rhetorical pattern the Create-a-Research-Space (or CARS) model.

Task One

Read our draft Introduction to our mini-RP and carry out the tasks that follow.

TABLE 21.   Moves in Research Paper Introductions

Move 1 *Context* *Background*	**Establishing a research territory** a. by showing that the general research area is important, central, interesting, problematic, or relevant in some way. (optional) b. by introducing and reviewing items of previous research in the area. (obligatory)
Move 2 *Need, gap*	**Establishing a niche[a]** *creating your research space* a. by indicating a gap in the previous research, raising a question about it, or extending previous knowledge in some way. (obligatory)
Move 3 *Purpose* *plan*	**Occupying the niche** *I'm going to fill in the space* a. by outlining purposes or stating the nature of the present research. (obligatory) b. by announcing principal findings. (optional) c. by indicating the structure of the RP. (optional) *→ obligatory*

[a] In ecology, a niche is a particular microenvironment where a particular organism can thrive. In our case, a niche is a context where a particular piece of research makes particularly good sense.

I.d. of the problem   a hole, a gap

The Position of Sentence Connectors in Academic English
C. B. Feak and J. M. Swales

Introduction

[1]Many commentators have noted that sentence connectors (e.g., *however*) are an important and useful element in expository and argumentative writing. [2]Frequency studies of their occurrence in academic English extend at least as far back as Huddleston (1971). [3]ESL writing textbooks have for many years regularly included chapters on sentence connectors (e.g., Herbert, 1965). [4]Most reference grammars deal with their grammatical status, classification, meaning, and use. [5]Some attention has also been given to the position of sentence connectors in clauses and sentences. [6]Quirk and Greenbaum (1973) observe (a) that the normal position is initial; (b) that certain connectors, such as *hence* and *overall*, "are restricted, or virtually restricted, to initial position" (p. 248); and (c) that medial positions are rare for most connectors, and final positions even rarer. [7]The only attempt known

niche

to us to explain differences in position on semantic grounds is an unpublished paper by Salera (1976) discussed in Celce-Murcia and Larsen-Freeman (1983). [8]The Salera paper deals only with adversatives like *however* and suggests that initial position reflects something contrary to expectation, while medial position reflects a contrast that is not necessarily unexpected. [9]However, neither of these studies provides any descriptive evidence of the actual positions of sentence connectors in academic texts. [10]In the present paper, we report on a preliminary study of sentence-connector position in a sample of twelve published articles.

1. Divide the text into the three basic moves.

2. Look at table 21 again. Where in our Introduction would you divide Move 1 into 1a and 1b?

3. What kind of Move 2 do we use? *Id of a gap*

4. What kind of Move 3a do we use?

5. Underline or highlight any words or expressions in sentences 1 through 3 used to establish a research territory.

6. List the six citations used in our draft introduction. (Salera is cited twice.) Do you have a criticism of our review of the previous literature?

7. Where do these six citations occur in the sentence? What does this tell us?

In Unit Seven, we argued that RPs were not simple accounts of investigations. This is also very true of our own mini-RP. If you look back at our introduction, you will note that we never actually say what our motive or rationale for carrying out this small study was. Rather, the study seems to emerge as a natural and rational response to a discovered gap in the literature.

In fact, this is not how the study started at all. In Fall 1992, a student in John's Research Paper Writing class asked him if there were any rules for where to put the sentence connectors. Not having any immediate answer, John played for time and asked what the class did. Most said they always put them first, even though they had noticed that they did not always come first in the books and papers that they read. Then one student, Arthur Hsieng, said that he remembered a sociology professor telling the class never to put *however* in initial position. As English teachers, we were so struck by this piece of grammatical folklore that we decided to investigate!

Task Two

Discuss the following issues with a group.

1. Do you think the "true" story behind our investigation should be built into the Introduction? If so, where and how?

2. Alternatively, do you think it should be made part of the Discussion? Or would the Acknowledgments be the best place to mention how the study came about? Or a footnote? Or should it be omitted altogether?

3. Do members of your group have comparable experiences to relate—perhaps stories about how pieces of research started almost by accident but are described as if they were planned?

4. How would you answer the following question? In any investigation, certain events take place in a certain order. Do you think it is necessary to keep to that order when writing an RP, or is an author free to change that order to construct a more rhetorically effective paper?

Of course, by this time you may be thinking that all this rhetorical work in Introductions is only needed in the social sciences and the humanities. There, academics may indeed need to create research spaces for themselves. Surely, you may be thinking, the CARS model is not necessary in "true" science. Before coming to any such conclusion, consider the first half of the Introduction to this paper from aerospace and atmospheric science.

X general subfield

Y sub- subfield

Z Problem, issue, crisis

High Angle-of-Attack Calculations of the
Sub-sonic Vortex Flow in Slender Bodies
D. Almosino

M
O
V
E
O
N
E

1a

1b

[1]The increasing interest in high angle-of-attack aerodynamics has heightened the need for computational tools suitable to predict the flowfield and the aerodynamic coefficients in this regime. [2]Of particular interest and complexity are the symmetric and asymmetric separated vortex flows which develop about slender bodies as the angle of attack is increased. [3]The viscous influence on the separation lines and the unknown three-dimensional (3D) shape of the vortex wake are some of the main flow features that must be modeled in the construction of a computational method to properly treat this problem. [4]Among the many potential flow methods developed in attempting to solve body vortex flows are early two dimensional (2D) multivortex methods,[2-4] 2D timestepping vortex models that include boundary-layer considerations,[5-8] and a quasi 3D potential flow method[9] that uses source and vortex elements. . . . [5]The potential flow methods are of special interest because of their ability to treat 3D body shapes and their separated vortex flows using a simple and relatively inexpensive model.

(Copyright © 1984 AIAA—Reprinted
with permission)

Find the three uses of *interest* in this passage. What does this tell us? What might the author say in sentence 6?

Language Focus: Claiming Centrality

Note particularly the language used in the first two sentences to express Move 1a.

The increasing interest in . . . has heightened the need for . . .
Of particular interest and complexity are . . . (This second sen-

tence uses the emphatic inversion discussed in the Language Focus on pages 144–47.)

Here are some further "skeletal" examples of these strong opening statements. Notice how many of them use the present perfect.

Recently, there has been growing interest in . . .
The possibility of . . . has generated wide interest in . . .
The development of . . . is a classic problem in . . .
The development of . . . has led to the hope that . . .
The . . . has become a favorite topic for analysis . . .
Knowledge of . . . has a great importance for . . .
The study of . . . has become an important aspect of . . .
A central issue in . . . is . . .
The . . . has been extensively studied in recent years.
Many investigators have recently turned to . . .
The relationship between . . . has been investigated by many researchers.
Many recent studies have focused on . . .

Task Three

Find a recent journal from your field of interest. Look at the openings of up to six articles. All the articles should come from the same journal. How many, if any, begin with a Move 1a? If any do, photocopy the openings or write them down and bring them to class. (Or send them to your instructor on electronic mail.)

Reviewing the Literature

The CARS model states that Move 1b (introducing and reviewing items of previous research in the area) is obligatory. Why should it be obligatory?

Task Four

There are, in fact, a surprisingly large number of theories about the role and purpose of citations in academic texts. Six are given here.

Discuss with a group the validity of each. Which do you think contribute most to our understanding of why citations are used in academic writing? Does your group have any other theories?

1. This theory is widely proposed in manuals and standard practice guides.

   Citations are used to recognize and acknowledge the intellectual property rights of authors. They are a matter of ethics and a defense against plagiarism (see Notes on Plagiarism in Unit Five).

2. This theory has many supporters, especially in well-established fields like the sciences.

   Citations are used to show respect to previous scholars. They recognize the history of the field by acknowledging previous achievements.

The remaining theories have been proposed by individual authors.

3. Ravetz 1971:

   Citations operate as a kind of mutual reward system. Rather than pay other authors money for their contributions, writers "pay" them in citations.

4. Gilbert 1977:

   Citations are tools of persuasion; writers use citations to give their statements greater authority.

5. Bavelas 1978:

   Citations are used to supply evidence that the author qualifies as a member of the chosen scholarly community; citations are used to demonstrate familiarity with the field.

6. Swales 1990:

> Citations are used to create a research space for the citing author. By describing what has been done, citations point the way to what has not been done and so prepare a space for new research.

Now suppose that we have actually carried out a study of the reasons for using citations in academic texts and have begun to write an RP. This is the draft of the introduction so far. Read it and consider the questions that follow.

M	[1]Citations are widely recognized as being an important
O	and distinctive property of academic texts. [2]Indeed, the
V	presence or absence of citations allows the casual reader
E	to get an immediate sense of whether a text is an "aca-
	demic" or "popular" one. [3]Because citation is such an ob-
1a	vious surface phenomenon, it has been much discussed in
	the academic world. [4]Indeed, there are several theories
	about the role and purpose of citations in academic texts.

We now have to write Move 1b.

1. How can we sequence our six theories (plus any others that have come up in your groups)? The key element in literature reviews is that *order* is imposed on the material, not so much order in your own mind, but order in the reader's mind.

2. Clearly we need to start with the two major traditional views (theories 1 and 2). How can we order the remaining four (3–6)?

3. Should we organize in the chronological order as presented? Is this—at least in this case—a weak kind of ordering? Is there another way?

4. One possibility might be to *categorize* theories 3–6. Do you consider the theories by Ravetz, Gilbert, Bavelas, and Swales to be

economic theories?
sociological theories?
rhetorical theories?

We could then decide to take next the case where we have two
members in the category. One plan could look like this.

Theory 1	
	Established major theories
Theory 2	

Rhetorical	Theories 4 and 6	Theories associated
Economic	Theory 3	with individual authors.
Sociological	Theory 5	

Task Five

Write either a short review of the citation literature or a short review of at least five papers from your own field. Use the reference
system that you are most comfortable with. If you review papers
from your field, also hand in a rough diagram showing how you have
imposed order on the material.

Language Focus: Citation and Tense

Tense choice in reviewing previous research is subtle and somewhat
flexible. (It is also not very much like the "rules" you may have been
taught in English classes.) The following, therefore, are only general
guidelines for tense usage.

Several studies have shown that at least two-thirds of all citing
statements fall into one of these three major patterns.

I. Past—researcher activity as agent

Jones (1987) *investigated* the causes of illiteracy.
The causes of illiteracy *were investigated* by Jones (1987).

II. Present Perfect—researcher activity not as agent

The causes of illiteracy *have been* widely *investigated* (Jones 1987, Ferrara 1990, Hyon 1994).
There *have been* several investigations into the causes of illiteracy (Jones 1987, Ferrara 1990, Hyon 1994).
Several researchers *have studied* the causes of illiteracy. [1-3]

III. Present—no reference to researcher activity

The causes of illiteracy *are* complex (Jones 1987, Ferrara 1990, Hyon 1994).
Illiteracy *appears to have* a complex set of causes. [1-3]

Note these common uses of these patterns:

Pattern I—reference to single studies—past
Pattern II—reference to areas of inquiry—present perfect
Pattern III—reference to state of current knowledge—present

[handwritten annotation: low status high]

Also note that in patterns I and II, attention is given to what previous researchers did, while in pattern III, the focus is on what has been found.

Finally note that different areas of scholarship have somewhat different preferences. Patterns I and II are most common in the humanities and least common in science, engineering, and medical research. However, all three patterns tend to occur in many extensive literature reviews, since they add *variety* to the text.

We have said that these three patterns cover about two-thirds of the cases. The reason this proportion is not higher is because writers of literature reviews can have certain options in their choice of tenses. This is particularly true of pattern I. The main verbs in pattern I can refer to what a previous researcher *did* (*investigated, studied, analyzed,* etc.). By and large, in these cases the past is obligatory. However, the main verbs can also refer to what the previous researcher *wrote* or *thought* (*stated, concluded, claimed,* etc.). With these reporting verbs, tense options are possible.

Jones (1987) concluded that illiteracy can be related to . . . *(specific work in 1987)*
Jones (1987) has concluded that . . . *(I'm interest in all his thinking (work))*
Jones (1987) concludes that . . .

The differences among these tenses are subtle. In general, a move from past to present perfect and then to present indicates that the research reported is increasingly *close* to the writer in some way: close to the writer's own opinion, close to the writer's own research, or close to the current state of knowledge.

The present tense choice is sometimes called the *citational present* and is also used with famous or important sources.

Plato argues that . . .
Confucius says . . .
The Bible says . . .
The Constitution states . . .

stated - de-emphasize
Comparable options exist in the subordinate clause.

(emphasize)
Jones (1987) found that illiteracy *was* correlated most closely with poverty.
Jones (1987) found that illiteracy *is* correlated most closely with poverty.

The first sentence shows that the writer believes that the finding should be understood within the context of the single study. In the second, the writer implies that a wider generalization is possible.

Variation in Reviewing the Literature

In the language focus, we concentrated on the three main citation patterns. There are, of course, some others.

According to Jones (1987), the causes of illiteracy are closely related to poverty.

Jones' research shows that illiteracy and poverty are inter-related (Jones 1987).

Can you come up with some more?

Good writers of literature reviews employ a range of patterns in order to vary their sentences. As this is something that we have already discussed in Task Twelve of Unit Six, you may want to review that section before doing this next task.

Task Six

Here is a review that uses only citation pattern I. As you can see, using the same structure all the time can cause the reader to lose interest. Rewrite the passage so that it has more variety. Your version will probably be shorter than the original—another advantage!

The Origins of the First Scientific Articles

past tense → past history

[1]The first scientific journal was started in London in 1665. [2]Obviously, the first scientific articles had no direct models to build on, and several scholars have discussed possible influences. [3]Ard (1983) suggests that the first articles developed from the scholarly letters that scientists were accustomed to sending to each other. [4]Sutherland (1986) showed that early articles were also influenced by the newspaper reports of that time. [5]Paradis (1987) described the influence of the philosophical essay. [6]Shapin (1984) claimed that the scientific books of Robert Boyle were another model. [7]Finally, Bazerman (1988) argued that discussion among the scientists themselves made its own contribution to the emergence of the scientific article.

Move 2—Establishing a Niche

In many ways, Move 2 is the key move in Introductions. It is the hinge that connects Move 1 (what has been done) to Move 3 (what the present research is about). Move 2 thus establishes the motivation for the study. By the end of Move 2, the reader should have a good idea of what is going to come in Move 3.

Most Move 2s establish a niche by indicating a gap—by showing that the research story so far is not yet complete. Move 2s then are a particular kind of critique (see Unit 6).

Usually Move 2s are quite short, often consisting of no more than a sentence. Sometimes, however, Move 2s can be quite complicated. Consider, for example, the Move 2 from the Almosino paper on the calculation of vortex flows. (Move 1 appears earlier in this unit.)

Task Seven

Read the middle section of the Almosino introduction (containing Move 2) and then answer the questions that follow.

Shift

M
O
V
E

2

[6]However, the previously mentioned methods suffer from some limitations mainly concerning the treatment of the vortex wake formation and its interaction with the body. [7]The first group of methods[2–4] cannot treat 3D flows and is limited to very slender bodies. [8]The second group of computational methods[5–8] is time consuming and therefore expensive, and its separation prediction is not sufficiently accurate. [9]Both the methods in this group and the method in[9] suffer from the dependency on too many semi-empirical inputs and assumptions concerning the vortex wake and its separation. [10]The steady, 3D nonlinear vortex-lattice method, upon which the present method is based, eliminates many of these limitations by introducing a more consistent model, but it can treat only symmetrical flow cases.

(Copyright © 1984 AIAA—Reprinted with permission)

1. How many "critique" expressions can you find in the passage? Underline or highlight them.

2. What word signals that Move 1 has ended and Move 2 has started? What other words or expressions could also indicate this shift?

3. This Move 2 occupies five sentences. Why do you think Almosino has put these sentences in this particular order?

4. What do you think the next sentence is going to be?

As we have seen, Almosino relies mostly on verbs and adjectives to characterize weaknesses in the previous research. Care is obviously needed when selecting vocabulary of this sort.

Task Eight

Here are some "negative" verbs and adjectives. Decide how "negative" they are. Work with a partner. Use the key below.

definitely or strongly negative = − −
neutral or slightly negative = −

Verbs

However, previous research in this field has _____.

−	a. concentrated on x.	−	g. neglected to consider x.
− −	b. disregarded x.	−	h. overestimated x.
− −	c. failed to consider x.	−	i. overlooked x.
−	d. ignored x.	−	j. been restricted to x.
−	e. been limited to x	−	k. suffered from x.
−	f. misinterpreted x.	−	l. underestimated x.

Adjectives

Nevertheless, these attempts to establish a link between secondary smoke and lung cancer are at present _____.

−	a. controversial	−	e. questionable
−	b. incomplete	−	f. unconvincing
−	c. inconclusive	−	g. unsatisfactory
−	d. misguided		

Language Focus: Negative Openings

Probably the most common way to indicate a gap is to use a "negative" subject. Presumably, negative subjects are chosen because they signal immediately to the reader that Move 1 has come to an end. Note the following uses of *little* and *few*:

Uncountable   However,   little information . . .   *less*
little attention . . .
little work . . .
little data . . .
little research . . .   (fewer)

Countable   However,   few studies . . .
few investigations . . .
few researchers . . .
few attempts . . .

Note the differences in the following pairs:

He has little research experience. (negative, i.e., not enough)
He has a little research experience. (neutral, i.e., maybe enough)

The department has few computers. (negative, i.e., not enough)
The department has a few computers. (neutral, i.e., maybe
    enough)

Note the use of *no/none of*:

    No studies/data/calculations . . .

Use *no* when your conclusion is based on but does not directly refer to the cited literature. If you want to refer directly to the previous research, use *none of*.

    singular
    None of these studies/findings/calculations . . .

Of course, not all RP Introductions express Move 2 by indicating an obvious gap. You may prefer, for various reasons, to avoid negative or quasi-negative comment altogether. In such cases, a useful alternative is to use a contrastive statement.

The research has tended to focus on . . . , rather than on . . .
These studies have emphasized . . . , as opposed to . . .
Although considerable research has been devoted to . . . , rather less attention has been paid to . . .

Two other strategies are quite common, particularly in the "harder" areas. The first is raising a question, a hypothesis, or a need. Here are some skeletal examples.

However, it remains unclear whether . . .
It would thus be of interest to learn how . . .
If these results could be confirmed, they would provide strong evidence for . . .
These findings suggest that this treatment might not be so effective when applied to . . .
It would seem, therefore, that further investigations are needed in order to . . .

Note that in these cases, sentence connectors are not limited to the *however* type.

The second strategy is continuing a line of research. This last strategy is largely restricted to RPs written by research groups who are following up their own research or that done by similar groups. The authors draw a conclusion from their survey of the previous research indicating how some finding in the immediate research literature can be extended or applied in some way. Here are three examples.

These recent developments in computer-aided design clearly have considerable potential. In this paper, we demonstrate . . .
The literature shows that Rasch Analysis is a useful technique for validating multiple-choice tests. This paper uses Rasch Analysis to . . .
Such active-R networks eliminate the need for any external passive reactance elements. This paper utilizes the active-R approach for the design of a circuit . . .

Occupying the Niche

The third and final step in the typical RP Introduction is to make an offer to fill the gap (or answer the question) that has been created in Move 2. The first element in Move 3 is obligatory. It has two main variants:

Purposive (P)   The author or authors indicate their main purpose or purposes.

or

Descriptive (D)   The author or authors describe the main feature of their research.

Task Nine

Here are the beginning parts of ten opening Move 3 sentences. Decide in each case whether they are purposive or descriptive, and enter a *P* or a *D* in the blank. One of them is from the Almosino paper (see Move 2 in Task Seven). Can you guess which one it is? Complete at least three of the sentences with your own words.

_P_ 1. The aim of the present paper is to give . . .

_D_ 2. This paper reports on the results obtained . . .

_D_ 3. In this paper we give preliminary results for . . .

_P_ 4. The main purpose of the experiment reported here was to . . .

_P_ 5. This study was designed to evaluate . . .

_D_ 6. The present work extends the use of the last model by . . .

_D_ 7. We now report the interaction between . . .

_P/D_ 8. The primary focus of this paper is on . . .

P
 9. The aim of this investigation was to test . . .

P
 10. It is the purpose of the present paper to provide . . .

Note that Move 3 is typically signaled by some reference to the present text, such as the uses of *this, the present, reported,* and *here.* If the conventions of the field or journal allow it, it is also common for the authors to switch from the impersonal to the personal by using *we,* or more rarely *I.* Also note that these signals come early in the sentence. It is very unusual to find:

We present the results of three experiments *in this paper.*

rather than:

In this paper we present the results of three experiments.

Language Focus: Tense and Purpose Statements

Students sometimes ask whether they should use *was* or *is* in purpose statements. Indeed, both were used in the phrases in Task Nine. The answer to this question depends on how you refer to your work. You have two choices:

1. Referring to the type of *text*—paper, article, thesis, report, research note, etc.
2. Referring to the type of *investigation*—experiment, investigation, study, survey, etc.

If you choose to refer to the type of text, you must use the present tense. If you write, "The aim of this paper was to . . . ," it suggests that you are referring to an original aim that has now changed.

If you choose to refer to the type of investigation, you can use either *was* or *is.* However, there is an increasing tendency to choose the present, perhaps because it makes the research seem relevant and fresh and new. The "safe rule" then is to opt for the present.

Completing an Introduction

There are a number of elements that can follow the purposive/descriptive statement. While these elements are typically needed in longer texts, such as theses, dissertations, or long and complex RPs, they may not be necessary in short RPs. We briefly review each in turn.

Secondary Aims or Features

Sometimes a second sentence is necessary to complete Move 3a. Here, for example, is the Almosino Move 3.

M [11]The present work extends the use of the last model to
O asymmetric, body-vortex cases, thus increasing the range
V of flow patterns that can be investigated. [12]In addition, an
E effort is made to improve the numerical procedure to accelerate the convergence of the iterative solution and to get a
3 better rollup of the vortex lines representing the wake.
(Copyright © 1984 AIAA—Reprinted with permission)

I spend some time on it, but not the main goal
(attempt)
→ Secondary thing

These secondary statements are often introduced by such language as

In addition, . . .
Additionally, . . .
A secondary aim . . .
A further reason for . . .

Stating Value

You may also want to consider whether you want to mention at this stage anything about the contribution your research will make. Of course, you will do this in the Discussion section in any case. Note that Almosino squeezes a value statement into his introduction.

. . . , thus increasing the range of flow problems that can be investigated.

If you opt for a value statement, it would be wise to be cautious and to use qualifications (see Unit Four).

Task Ten

At present the Feak and Swales draft Introduction (see Task One) simply ends with a Move 3a.

> In the present paper, we report on a preliminary study of sentence-connector position in a sample of twelve published articles.

Would you advise us to add any of the following value statements? What are the advantages or disadvantages of each? If you do not like any of them, can you offer one of your own, or edit one of them to your satisfaction? Work with a partner if possible.

1. In this way, we offer a solution to a long-standing problem in English grammar.

2. It is hoped that this small study will revive interest in a long-neglected feature of academic English.

3. The information presented should be useful to all those teaching academic writing to nonnative speakers of English.

Announcing Principal Findings

There is some confusion as to whether RP Introductions should close with a statement of the principal results. One investigation (Swales and Najjar 1987) found that physicists do this about half the time, but educational researchers hardly ever include such statements. One useful guideline is to ask yourself whether the RP will open with an Abstract. If there is an Abstract, do you need to give the main findings three times: in the Abstract, in the Introduction and in the Results? We think not. If there is no Abstract, you may wish to reconsider. Another suggestion would be to follow standard practice in your field—or ask your instructor.

Outlining the Structure of the Text

A final option is to consider whether you need to explain how your text is organized. This element is obligatory in dissertations, but is only included in RPs under certain circumstances. One such circumstance arises when your text is unusual in some way, such as not using the IMRD format. Another arises if you are working in some new field. Cooper (1985) found, for example, that outlining the RP structure was quite common in computer technology. Ask yourself whether your anticipated readers need to have the organization of the RP explained.

Here is a useful example of a textual outline, well-motivated by the unusual structure of the paper. Notice how it uses a good variety of sentence structures. The paper is about currency rates in the European Common Market and was written by one of our students.

> The plan of this paper is as follows. Section II describes the current arrangements for regulating exchange rates within the EC. In Section III a theoretical model is constructed which is designed to capture these arrangements. Experimental parameters are then tested in Section IV. Finally, Section V offers some suggestions for the modification of the current mechanisms.
>
> (Pierre Martin, unedited)

Task Eleven

Below is a textual outline by another one of our students. Notice how this time it lacks variety. Can you rewrite it?

> The rest of the paper is organized as follows. Section 2 presents the theoretical concept. Section 3 presents the empirical specification, the implementation of the model. Section 4 presents the results of statistical and other computational analyses. Section 5 summarizes the findings and provides a brief discussion concerning the shortcomings of the methods employed. Finally, an appendix presenting the detailed algebraic works is presented at the end of the paper.
>
> (Abdul Malik, unedited)

Task Twelve

Now write, or rewrite, an RP introduction of your own.

Discussion Sections

It is not so easy to provide useful guidelines for writing Discussion or Conclusions sections. (We will not distinguish between these two terms, since the difference is largely conventional, depending on traditions in particular fields and journals.) See what is done in your own field.

The problem is that Discussions vary considerably depending on a number of factors. Not all these factors are understood, but one important one is the kind of research question—or questions—that the study attempted to answer. Another factor that leads to variation is the position of the Discussion section in the RP. By the time readers reach the Discussion, authors can assume a fair amount of shared knowledge. They can assume (if not always correctly) that the reader has understood the purpose of the study, obtained a sense of the methodology, and followed along with the results. Authors can use this understanding to pick and choose what to concentrate on in the Discussion. As a result, they typically have greater freedom than in the Introduction.

Overall, if Results deal with *facts*, then Discussions deal with *points*; facts are *descriptive*, while points are *interpretive*. Effective Discussion sections are similar to effective lectures, which, as Olsen and Huckin (1990) note, are based on points, rather than on facts. Further, authors of Discussions have some flexibility in deciding which of their possible points to include and then which to highlight.

Discussions, then, should be more than summaries. They should go beyond the results. They should be

P₁ Purpose

P₂ Plan

F Finding

O Organization

Discussion
Remarks
Summary
Conclusion

more theoretical
or
more abstract
or
more general
or   AND, if possible, some
more integrated with the field   combination of these.
or
more connected to the real world
or
more concerned with implications
or applications

As Weissberg and Buker note, "in the discussion section you should step back and take a broad look at your findings and your study as a whole" (1990, 160).

We have said that Discussions can be viewed as presenting a series of points. Typically, they are arranged as in table 22.

Move 1 is usually quite extensive, and Moves 2 and 3 are often quite short. At this point, you might want to observe that Move 1 and the later moves seem self-contradictory. Why, you may ask, build up something in order to apparently attack it later? However, if we remember *positioning*, we can see that authors can present themselves very effectively by both

1. highlighting intelligently the strengths of the study
   and
2. highlighting intelligently its weaknesses.

Indeed, Moves 2 and 3 can also be used to identify and open up future research space for authors and their colleagues. However,

TABLE 22.   Discussion Moves

Move 1	Points to consolidate your research space (obligatory)
Move 2	Points to indicate the limitations of your study (optional but common)
Move 3	Points to identify useful areas of further research (optional and only common in some areas)

this is less likely to happen, according to Huckin (1987), in areas where there is fierce competition for research grants.

Task Thirteen

We have noted in this task nine points we would like to make in the Discussion section of the paper on sentence connectors. They are not yet in order. We believe that they fall in the following categories:

Move 1 (Consolidation)	Six Points (3 results, 1 methodology, 1 centrality, 1 literature comparison)
Move 2 (Limitation)	Two points
Move 3 (Further research)	One point

Into which category does each point fall? Fill in the blanks with the labels. The first one has been done for you. Review the Methods, Results, and Introduction sections of our mini-RP, if necessary (see Unit Seven and Unit Eight Task One). The first one has been done for you.

1. Move 2 (Limitation)
   This is a very limited study restricted to a single field.

2. _____
   Position varies from one connector to another (+ example[s]).

3. _____
   Sentence-connectors are quite common in academic writing (average of 2 per page).

4. _____
   Our survey shows unexpected differences in the frequency with which individual connectors are used (+ example[s]).

5. _____

Further research in this area might produce materials of greater help to writers, especially nonnative speakers.

6. _____

Our survey shows that 25% of connectors do not occur at the beginning of sentences.

7. _____

It is important to conduct surveys to establish where connectors actually occur in sentences.

8. _____

We are not yet in a position to offer explanations for choices of connector positions.

9. _____

Twenty-five percent noninitial seems higher than the grammar books would predict, but lower than Morrow (1989), who found 53% noninitial in an economics journal (although Morrow used a broader definition of connector).

As we can see, the heart of a Move 1 typically consists of statements of results followed by a follow-up of some kind. The follow-up might take the form of examples, comparisons with other work, conclusions that might be drawn, or commentary on whether the results are expected or unexpected.

Task Fourteen

Please write our Discussion section for us. Refer to the Results section before Task Five for details of our study.

Opening a Discussion Section

As we have already suggested, there are many options in opening a Discussion. Consider the case of the following data. We studied Discussion openings in 15 articles from a small U.S. regional journal of

[handwritten annotations:]
1. Summarize results
2. What do results suggest?
3. Unexpected outcomes
4. reference to previous research
5. claim about generalizability
6. Recommendations for further research

I Consolidation
examples
comparisons
conclusions
commentary

II limitations
III Recommendations

natural history research. We found great variation. Four sections open with the _main results_. This was the largest category, but still less than 30% of the total. Three begin with a _discussion of the literature._ Here are two examples.

a. Graikowski et al. (1986) recovered . . . toxin from . . . and found that . . . suffered 100% mortality when . . .
b. Food shortages, social stress . . . within . . . are causes of dispersal among . . . (Fritz and Mech 1981, Messier 1985, Mech 1987, Packard and Mech 1980).

Two sections start in a more dramatic way by offering a general conclusion.

c. Apparently, we are witness to the early phases of a classic population explosion.
d. From this data, it is clear that . . . are not major consumers of commercially important fish-species in . . .

The remaining types of opening occur only once in the sample. We were surprised, for example, to find only _one_ opening that reminds the reader of the _original purpose_.

e. The objective of the survey was to quar.tify the number of . . . within . . .

In another case, the author opens with _a summary._

f. This report brings together all known records of . . . since 1959.

In another, the authors raise the level of discussion by referring to _theory_.

g. The interrelationship of bird populations and the environment is extremely complex.

One author starts with a comment about _methodology._

h. There is a bias associated with using either ground or aerial counts, exclusively.

Another author begins his Discussion section by highlighting the special importance of his _research site._

i. ... is one of the few sites in North America where the presence of a significant number of migrating ... has been documented.

And in the final case, the author actually begins by discussing the _limitations_ of the data.

j. The census figure of ... is expected to be an underestimate of the total population of ...

This small survey shows some of the many strategies that can be adopted for opening a Discussion section. The choice of strategy clearly depends in part on how the authors view their work. We will briefly comment on the last three cases. In _h_ the author begins with a methodology critique of previous work, because one of his main points is that he has taken the trouble to "combine both aerial and ground surveys." In _i_ the researcher begins by stressing the point that the location of his research site offers exceptional advantages. Finally, take the case of _j_. It might appear that the author of _j_ has adopted a very risky strategy, but in this particular context it is not. It soon emerges that carrying out a complete census of this particular species would be very difficult. Therefore, the author presumably felt on safe ground when he opened in this way. Indeed, he can go on to claim that his numbers are much larger than anybody else has so far been able to report.

Task Fifteen

Survey and classify the openings of at least six Discussion sections from a journal in your field. Bring your findings to class.

Language Focus: Levels of Generalization

In the Results sections, statements may be quite specific and closely tied to the data.

As can be seen in Table 1, 84% of the students performed above the 12th-grade level.

Seven out of eight experimental samples resisted corrosion longer
than the controls.

On the other hand, in the Abstract or in a Summary section, space
restrictions may lead to a high level of generality.

The results indicate that the students performed above the 12th-
grade level.
The experimental samples resisted corrosion longer than the controls.

In the Discussion, we usually expect something in between these
two levels. One common device is to use one of the following "phrases
of generality."

Overall
In general
On the whole
In the main
With . . . exception(s)

Overall, the results indicate that students performed above the
12th-grade level.
The overall results indicate . . .
The results indicate, overall, that . . .

In general, the experimental samples resisted . . .
With one exception, the experimental samples resisted . . .

Ex. lg The questionnaire

Limitations in Discussions

We saw in Introduction Move 2s (see page 185–89) that extensive
"negative" language was a possible option. In contrast, Discussion
Move 2s tend to use less elaborate negative language. The main
reason is obvious; it is now your own research that you are talking
about! Another reason is that many limitation statements in Discussions are not so much about the weaknesses in the research, as
about what *cannot be concluded* from the study in question. Producing statements of this kind provides an excellent opportunity for the

writer to show that he or she understands how evidence needs to be evaluated in the particular field.

Task Sixteen

Complete four of the statements in set *A*. Base two on the mini-RP on sentence connectors and two on studies you have been involved with in your field. Complete at least one statement from B.

A. Limitations of Research Scope

    1. It should be noted that this study has examined only . . .
    2. This analysis has concentrated on . . .
    3. The findings of this study are restricted to . . .
    4. This study has addressed only the question of . . .
    5. The limitations of this study are clear: . . .
    6. We would like to point out that we have not . . .

B. Limitations in Conclusions. Below are some typical openings for statements that firmly state that certain conclusions should *not* be drawn.

    1. However, the findings do not imply . . .
    2. The results of this study cannot be taken as evidence for . . .
    3. Unfortunately, we are unable to determine from this data . . .
    4. The lack of . . . means that we cannot be certain . . .

We said earlier that Move 2s are optional in Discussions. If you feel it is unnecessary to comment on your work in either of the above two ways, a useful alternative is to place the limitation in an opening phrase.

Notwithstanding its limitations, this study does suggest . . .
Despite its preliminary character, the research reported here
    would seem to indicate . . .
However exploratory, this study may offer some insight into . . .

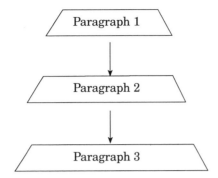

Fig. 11. Shape of a longer Discussion

Cycles of Moves

Finally, we should point out that many Discussion sections run through the Move 1-2-3 (or part of it) sequence more than once. Commonly, each cycle occupies one paragraph. Further, the more research questions there are to be discussed, the more this cycling is likely to occur. Such cycling can also occur in Introductions, but it tends to be less common, especially in shorter RPs.

If you wish to write a longer Discussion, follow the shape recommended in figure 11. Begin with specifics and then move towards the more general.

Task Seventeen

Write or rewrite a Discussion section for your own research. If you are working with others, collaborate with them.

Acknowledgments

Acknowledgments have become an integral part of most RPs. Indeed, one famous professor of our acquaintance reported to us that he always reads the Acknowledgments section of an RP first. When we asked him why, he replied, "Oh, the first thing I want to know is who has been talking to whom." While we do not think that this is standard reading behavior, it does show that Acknowledgments can be more than a display of necessary politeness.

Acknowledgments occur either at the bottom of the first page, following the Discussion, or sometimes at the end. They provide an opportunity for you to show that you are a member of a community and have benefited from that membership. Here we list some of the common elements in Acknowledgments.

1. Financial support

> Support for this work was provided by (sponsor).
> This research was partially supported by a grant from (sponsor).
> This research was funded by Contract (number) from (sponsor).

2. Thanks

> We would like to thank A, B, and C for their help . . .
> I wish to thank A for his encouragement and guidance throughout this project.
> We are indebted to B for . . .
> We are also grateful to D for . . .

3. Disclaimers (following element 1 or 2)

> However, the opinions expressed here do not necessarily reflect the policy of (sponsor).
> The interpretations in this paper remain my own.
> None, however, is responsible for any remaining errors.
> However, any mistakes that remain are my own.

4. Other versions

> An earlier/preliminary version of this paper was presented at (conference or seminar).

5. Source

> This article is based on the first author's doctoral dissertation.

This paper is based on research completed as partial fulfill-
ment for the Ph.D. requirements at (university name).

Notes

1. We believe that, if permitted, Acknowledgments should be written in the first person—*I* for a single author and *We* for coauthors. It
is possible to find phrases like "the present authors," but we consider
them too formal for this situation.

2. As far as we can see, financial support tends to come first,
followed by thanks. Disclaimers seem optional. Mentions of other
versions and sources (if used) seem to come either at the beginning
or at the end. (But note that, in theses or dissertations, it is customary to open with thanks to supervisors, advisors, committee-
members, etc.)

Task Eighteen

Write a suitable Acknowledgments section for one of your pieces of
work. If necessary, invent some forms of assistance to expand the
section.

Titles

Although the title comes first in an RP, it may sometimes be written
last. Its final form may be long delayed and much thought about and
argued over. Authors know that titles are important, they know that
the RP will be known by its title, and they know that a successful
title will attract readers while an unsuccessful one will discourage
readers.

What then are the requirements for good RP titles? In general, we
suggest the following three.

1. The title should indicate the topic of the study.
2. The title should indicate the scope of the study (i.e., neither
   overstating nor understating its significance).
3. The title should be self-explanatory to readers in the chosen
   area.

In some cases it may be helpful to also indicate the nature of the study (experiment, case report, survey, etc.), but this is not always required.

Notice that we have so far not mentioned the length of the title. The expected length of RP titles is very much a disciplinary matter. In some areas, such as the life sciences, titles are becoming longer and looking more and more like full sentences. In others, the preferred style is for short titles containing mostly nouns and prepositions.

Finally, at this stage in your career, we advise against "clever," "joke," or "trick" titles. These can be very successful for undergraduates and for senior scholars, but in your case, such titles may simply be interpreted as mistakes. Here is an example of such a title. The author of the paper is Professor Hartley, a well-known professor of psychology who conducted many experiments on what makes English texts easy or difficult to read. In this instance, he has been comparing texts that have "ragged right" at the end of the lines with those that are straight or "justified." Here is the title:

Unjustified Experiments in Typographical Research and Instructional Design. (*British Journal of Educational Technology* 2 [1973]: 120–31)

In this case, we can assume that Professor Hartley is making a joke. But if you wrote it?

As it happens, we have in this textbook already referred to a fair number of written texts, some written by our students, but most from published sources. Look at the titles of thirteen of them.

Are there any that appeal to you? Why?

1. Global Implications of Patent Law Variation (Suzuki, p. 110)
2. Mapping Dark Matter with Gravitational Lenses (Tyson, p. 117)
3. Blue Whale Population May Be Increasing off California (Boskin, p. 117)
4. Is There a Female Style in Science? (Barinaga, p. 117)
5. Reducing Air Pollution in Urban Areas: The Role of Urban Planners (Iseki, p. 124)
6. ESL Spelling Errors (Tesdell, p. 138)

7. Chinese EFL Students' Learning Strategies for Oral Communication (Huang, p. 142)
8. Rhetorical Patterns in English and Japanese (Kobayashi, p. 146)
9. The Position of Sentence Connectors in Academic English (Feak and Swales, p. 175)
10. High Angle-of-Attack Calculations of the Sub-sonic Vortex Flow in Slender Bodies (Almosino, p. 178)
11. Children's Punctuation: An Analysis of Errors in Period Placement (Cordeiro, p. 174)
12. On the Use of the Passive in Two Astrophysics Journal Papers (Tarone et al., p. 161)
13. Arguing for Experimental "Facts" in Science: A Study of Research Article Results Sections in Biochemistry (Thompson, p. 157)

Task Nineteen

Complete the analysis of these titles in table 23. Can you determine the system of capitalization that has been used in these titles? Is it the same as in your field? (Changes in capitalization occur in the reference list; see the notes at the beginning of our references on p. 247.)

You may have noticed that titles do not always follow the standard rules for using articles in English. Look again at titles 1 and 3. Are the articles sometimes omitted in your field?

As it happens, only two of the 13 titles use qualifications: Boskin (3) uses *may* and Tarone et al. (12) use *on*. What differences do you see between the following pairs of titles?

1a. On the Use of the Passive in Journal Articles
1b. The Use of the Passive in Journal Articles

2a. A Study of Research Article Results Sections
2b. A Preliminary Study of Research Article Results Sections

3a. An Analysis of Errors in Period Placement
3b. Toward an Analysis of Errors in Period Placement

TABLE 23. RP Title Analysis

Title	Number of words	Any verbs	Punctuation	Field
1	6	no	none	law
2		mapping		
3				
4				
5				
6				
7				
8				discourse analysis
9				
10				
11				
12				
13				

4a. The Role of Urban Planners
4b. The Potential Role of Urban Planners
4c. A Possible Role for Urban Planners

Depending on your field, you may wish to consider using qualifications in your titles. In nearly all cases, the process of arriving at the final form of a title is one of narrowing it down and making it more specific. Qualifications can be helpful in this process.

Table 23 in Task Nineteen reveals that three of the 13 titles use a colon.

  5. Reducing Air Pollution in Urban Areas: The Role of Urban Planners
 11. Children's Punctuation: An Analysis of Errors in Period Placement
 13. Arguing for Experimental "Facts" in Science: A Study of Research Article Results Sections in Biochemistry

Colons are widely used in titles, e.g., in the title of this book. One of the colon's typical functions is to separate ideas in such combinations as the following:

Before the Colon: After the Colon

Problem: Solution
General: Specific
Topic: Method
Major: Minor

Maybe you can think of others.

Task Twenty

Expand the following titles by adding a secondary element after the colon. Check back through the text where necessary (The page numbers are given in the list on pp. 206–7.)

1. Global Implications of Patent Law Variation:

6. ESL Spelling Errors:

7. Chinese EFL Students' Learning Strategies for Oral Communication:

8. Rhetorical Patterns in English and Japanese:

9. The Position of Sentence Connectors in Academic English:

Task Twenty-one

Bring the title of one of your papers to class and be prepared to discuss its final form and how it got there.

Abstracts

In this final section, we will work on two kinds of abstracts. First, we will work on abstracts to be placed at the beginning of an RP. In most situations, these will be abstracts based on texts that you have already written. Second, we will work on the conference abstract. In this case, you may or may not have a text to work from.

There is a third kind of abstract—the kind that occurs in an abstracting journal. Such abstracts often use special conventions and are typically written by professional abstractors. They will not concern us.

Research Paper Abstracts

RP abstracts usually consist of a single paragraph containing from about four to ten full sentences. This kind of abstract is more important for the reader than for the writer. By this we mean that an unsatisfactory RP abstract is not likely to affect whether the paper is finally accepted for publication (although the editors may suggest changes to it). It may, however, affect how many people will read your paper. We know from many studies that readers of academic journals employ a vast amount of skimming and scanning. If they like your abstract, they may read your paper, or at least part of it. If the do not like it, they may not.

There are two main approaches to writing RP abstracts. One we shall call the "results-driven" abstract, because it concentrates on the research findings and what might be concluded from them. The other approach is to offer an "RP summary" abstract in which you provide one- or two-sentence synopses of each of the four sections. In both cases, the abstracts will be either *informative* or *indicative* (see p. 81). Most RP abstracts should aim to be informative (i.e., they should include the main findings). However, this may not be possible with very long papers or with very theoretical ones (as in mathematics).

Task Twenty-two

Read the two drafts of the abstracts for our mini-RP. Then answer the questions that follow.

result – driven
Sample

Version A
results
Conclusion about area of study

A count of sentence connectors in 12 academic papers produced 70 different connectors. These varied in frequency from 62 tokens (*however*) to single occurrences. Seventy-five percent of the 467 examples appeared in sentence-initial position. However, individual connectors varied considerably in position preference. Some (e.g., *in addition*) always occurred initially; in other cases (e.g., *for example, therefore*), they were placed after the subject more than 50% of the time. These findings suggest that a search for general rules for connector position may not be fruitful.

niche – need, gap
sample

Version B
results
Conclusion about the diff. of research

Although sentence connectors are a well-recognized feature of academic writing, little research has been undertaken on their positioning. In this study, we analyze the position of 467 connectors found in a sample of 12 research papers. Seventy-five percent of the connectors occurred at the beginning of sentences. However, individual connectors varied greatly in positional preference. Some, such as *in addition,* only occurred initially; others, such as *therefore,* occurred initially in only 40% of the cases. These preliminary findings suggest that general rules for connector position will prove elusive.

Indirect

1. The journal requirements state that the abstracts accompanying papers should not exceed 100 words. Do versions *A* and *B* qualify?

2. Which version is "results driven" and which is an "RP summary"?

3. Compare the tense usage in versions A and B.

4. Which version do you prefer? And why?

5. Some journals also ask for a list of *key words*. Choose three or four suitable key words.

Language Focus: Linguistic Features of Abstracts

On the basis of her research into abstracts from a wide range of fields, Naomi Graetz (1985) gives these linguistic specifications as characteristic of abstracts:

1. the use of full sentences
2. the use of the past tense
3. the use of impersonal passive
4. the absence of negatives
5. the avoidance of "abbreviation, jargon, symbols and other language shortcuts that might lead to confusion."

Despite Graetz's second conclusion (abstracts use the past tense), it seems clear that tense usage in abstracts is fairly complicated. First, the conclusions are nearly always in the present. Second, RP summary abstracts often use the present or present perfect for their opening statements. Third, there appears to be considerable disciplinary and individual tense variation with sentences dealing with results.

In the versions in Task Twenty-two, the results were all expressed through the past tense. Nevertheless, it is not difficult to find exceptions to this pattern. Here is a short abstract from the Rapid Communications section of the journal *Physical Review A* (1993).

Nuclear-Structure Correction to the Lamb Shift
K. Pachucki, D. Leibfried, and T. W. Hänsch

[1]In this paper the second-order nuclear-structure correction to the energy of hydrogen-like systems is estimated and previous results are corrected. [2]Both deuterium and hydrogen are considered. [3]In the case of deuterium the correction is proportional to the nuclear polarizability and amounts to about -19kHz for the 1S state. [4]For hydrogen the resulting energy shift is about -60Hz.

Our investigations suggest that the shift to the present tense is more likely to occur in physical sciences such as physics, chemistry, and astrophysics and less likely to occur in the social sciences. We also found that physicists and chemists were—perhaps surprisingly— more likely to adopt a personal stance. Indeed, we have found occasional abstracts, particularly in astrophysics, which contain sequences of sentence openings like the following:

We discuss . . .
We compute . . .
We show . . .
We argue . . .
We conclude . . .

It would therefore seem that choice of tense and person may again be partly a strategic matter in abstracts. Choosing the present tense option—if permitted—can produce an effect of liveliness and contemporary relevance. Choosing *we* can add pace, by making the abstract a little shorter.

Task Twenty-three

Analyze five abstracts from a central journal in your field in terms of the five characteristics proposed by Graetz. To what extent do your findings agree with hers? Be prepared to summarize your findings in class, perhaps in the form of a table.

Conference Abstracts

This second type of abstract is somewhat different from the RP abstract. It is usually much longer; most of a page rather than a single paragraph (and can be even longer, especially in engineering). It is independent; in other words, whether you are accepted for the conference program depends entirely on how your conference abstract is perceived by the review panel. Your primary audience is, therefore, the conference reviewing committee. Appealing to the conference participants is a secondary consideration. At the beginning of this section, we mentioned another difference: it is very possible that you do not yet have a text to construct your abstract out of. Finally, it is also possible that you have not yet completed all the work for your RP. For example, you might have three experiments planned, but as the deadline descends on you, you have results from only two of them. In effect, your abstract may not be entirely *informative*.

In consequence of these and other factors, conference abstracts are much more of "a selling job" than RP abstracts. As a result, most conference abstracts have an opening section that attempts to

- create a research space,
- impress the review committee, and
- appeal (if accepted) to as large an audience as possible.

Task Twenty-four

Here are two successful conference abstracts written by two of our students. The versions presented are at least third drafts. The first is from music theory and the second from business management. Read them and carry out the tasks that follow.

Rhythm, Meter, and the Notated Meter in Webern's
Variations for Piano, Op. 27

[1]One of the problematic issues in post-tonal music is the notion of rhythm and meter. [2]In the numerous analyses of Webern's Variations for Piano, Op. 27, analysts have failed to agree about the role of the notated meter in the rhythmic and metrical structure

of the piece. [3]Some claim the notated meter to be purely conventional and not to be observed in performance, while others give an alternative changing meter to the one notated. [4]This paper seeks to illustrate that the notion of rhythm and meter in Webern's Op. 27 is a delicate and, more significantly, an intentional interplay between the notated meter, and the rhythm and meter arising from the phrase structure of the piece. [5]In order to demonstrate this, the paper presents an analysis examining the phrase structure of the piece, seeing it as an interaction between the pitch and the rhythmic domain. [6]The analysis employs the concept of Generalized Musical Intervals (GIS) developed by Lewin, as well as applications of the traditional notion of phrase rhythm. [7]These features are then presented in interaction with the row structure of the piece. [8]The paper closes by suggesting that an essential feature in understanding rhythm and meter in Webern's Op. 27 is the interaction between the various layers of the music: that is, the underlying row structure, the surface interpretation of the row structure, the phrase rhythm, the meter, and the notated meter.

(Tiina Koivisto, very minor editing)

Speed and Innovation in Cross-functional Teams

[1]The competitive and uncertain business environment of the 1990s requires an accelerated product development process with greatly improved coordination and integration among cross-functional teams (Denison, Kahn and Hart 1991). [2]Their successful product development effort suggests that speed and variety in perspective and expertise are compatible. [3]Although product development using cross-functional teams has been drawing much attention from academics as well as the corporate world, research into its organization and processes is still underdeveloped. [4]This deficiency is significant because the traditional literature on decision making has assumed that speed and variety are, in reality, incompatible. [5]This paper elaborates the process of cross-functional team efforts, based on interviews and observations over a two-year period. [6]A model is developed and operationalized with 22 survey measures and tested with data from 183 individuals on 29 teams. [7]Results show that product development using

cross-functional teams is highly correlated with time compression, creativity, capability improvement, and overall effectiveness.

(Kaz Ichijo, very minor editing)

1. Underline all instances in the two texts where the authors use evaluative language to strengthen their case for the acceptability of their research.

2. Circle all instances of metadiscourse (i.e., when the authors talk about their own texts). What difference do you see between the two authors?

3. Where are the divisions between the "scene setting" and the actual studies in these two texts? Do the proportions of each surprise you?

4. Why do you think the two abstracts were accepted? Were the reasons similar in each case?

5. Where do you suppose the students were in their studies when they wrote their conference abstracts? Circle your guess.
In Tiina's case:

a. All the work had been completed.
b. All but part of the analysis of the row structure had been done.
c. She had studied GIS, but had only tried it out on small samples.

In Kaz's case:

a. Almost everything had been done.
b. All the data had been collected and analyzed, but the model was not yet developed.
c. The data had been collected, but only analyzed in a preliminary way in order to get a sense of where it was going.

Citations in Conference Abstracts

In many cases, a conference abstract is read and assessed fairly quickly—maybe in only a few minutes. Under these conditions it does no harm to try to indicate at the beginning that you understand what is going on in your own specialized area. For that reason, many conference abstracts contain one or two carefully selected references to recent literature. In this way, authors can communicate that they are in touch with the latest developments. However, as Tiina's abstract shows, it is not always necessary or even desirable to give the citations in full.

Task Twenty-five

Your advisor contacts you about an upcoming small regional conference and suggests that you submit a conference abstract based on your current work. The deadline is ten days away. The abstracts should be anonymous and between 150 and 200 words. Make sure you have a draft ready for your next writing class.

Appendixes

Appendix One
Articles in Academic Writing

Three of the most common words in the English language are also three of the most difficult to use. We are referring to the articles *a*, *an*, and *the*. We will not attempt here to give you every rule of article use in English, but we will provide you with a quick review of some basic rules to guide you in your choice of *a*, *an*, *the*, and ∅ (no article needed). For a much more complete discussion of article use in academic writing, we suggest you look at Peter Master's *Science, Medicine, and Technology: English Grammar and Technical Writing*.

1. Countability

Before deciding if you should use an article, you should determine whether the noun in question is countable or uncountable, and whether it is generic (representative or symbolic) or specific (actual). Let us first take a look at specific nouns and countability. We will take a look at generic use in section 5 of this appendix.

Task One

Mark the following nouns as either countable (C) or uncountable (U).

commodity	——	money	——
complication	——	problem	——
computer	——	progress	——
device	——	proposal	——
discrepancy	——	research	——
energy	——	research project	——
equipment	——	researcher	——
fracture	——	society	——
information	——	theory	——
knowledge	——	traffic	——
machinery	——	vegetation	——
model	——	work	——

Determining whether a noun is countable may not be as easy as it seems. First, you cannot tell whether a noun is countable simply by looking at it. Some nouns that you intuitively think can be counted may not be countable. Money, for example, can be counted; however, the noun *money* itself is uncountable. If you do not know whether a noun is countable, you can either ask a native speaker or check a dictionary. (If a plural form is given, it is usually countable.) Second, a noun that is countable in one language may not be countable in another and vice versa. *Information*, for example, is uncountable in English but countable in most of its European equivalents. The following nouns are usually uncountable in English.

Names for languages—Chinese, Korean, French, Arabic . . .
Names for areas of study—physics, biology, economics . . .
Names for solids—coal, steel, marble . . .
Names for liquids—water, nitric acid, oil . . .
Names for gases—oxygen, hydrogen, methane . . .
Names for powders—salt, sugar, sand . . .

Third, although you may have learned that nouns are either countable or uncountable, this is not the whole story. There are quite a number of nouns that can be either. These can be referred to as *double nouns*. There may even be considerable differences in meaning between the countable noun and its uncountable counterpart. Table 24 lists some double nouns. An important group of nouns in this category refers to concepts that can be measured or quan-

TABLE 24.   Double Nouns

Uncountable	Countable
analysis (in general)	an analysis (a particular one)
calculation (in general)	a calculation (a particular one)
diamond (the hard substance)	a diamond (a precious stone)
iron (the substance)	an iron (a device for ironing)
science (in general)	a science (a particular one)
grain (in general), i.e., cereal	a grain (a particular one), i.e., a grain of salt

tified. Examples of these are *temperature, pressure, voltage, growth, density,* and *velocity.* Can you describe the difference between *temperature* and *a temperature* in the following sentences?

A thermometer measures *temperature.*
Temperature is expressed in degrees.
A *temperature* of over 120°C was recorded.
The patient ran a high *temperature* for several days.

Fourth, some nouns that are almost always uncountable in everyday English may have countable uses in technical English. Can you explain the difference in usage between the italicized nouns in the following sentences?

Rice is a staple food around the world.
A *rice* that can resist certain types of diseases should be introduced to the farmers of the region.

Steel is critical for the construction of skyscrapers.
The use of a light-weight *steel* would improve fuel efficiency.

There are at least two possible explanations for the difference. One is that the second sentence of each set involves a highly specialized use of the term that would most likely only be used by experts in the field who may find it necessary to make such fine distinctions. For example, while most nonexperts would make a distinction between rice and wheat or between steel and aluminum, they would not necessarily distinguish between different types of rice or steel. Experts, however, can and do. Another reason may be for purposes of conciseness. It is simply more efficient for experts to talk of *steels* rather than *different types of steel.* (However, we recommend that you do not shift uncountable nouns to countable unless you have seen examples from your field of study.)

Finally, some nouns in English are perhaps in the process of shifting from uncountable to countable. For instance, although *work* has long been an uncountable noun, it is not unusual to hear students say that they have "a lot of homeworks to do." Further, *research* is an uncountable noun for the vast majority of native speakers; however, it is not at all inconceivable that it may someday become countable—perhaps as a result of pressure from nonnative speakers.

Once you have determined what type of noun you are using, you then can make some further decisions regarding your choice (or omission) of article.

2. The Indefinite Article and $\varnothing$

A(n) and *one* are related but not identical. As you know, a(n) indicates that the noun is *any* single item, rather than a specific one. A(n), therefore, can *never* be used with plural or uncountable nouns. A is used before consonant sounds, while *an* is used before vowel sounds. Sound, not spelling, is important here. Notice the difference between *an uprising* and *a university.*

A(n) is typically used with the first mention of a singular countable noun, but not always. There are a number of linguistic contexts that require the use of *the*. (See section 3.)

Usually, no article ($\varnothing$) is necessary for the first mention of a plural or an uncountable noun where none of the special conditions for definite article use apply. (See section 3.)

3. The Definite Article

The use of the definite article is far more problematic than the use of the indefinite, because the definite article is used in a number of different ways. The most important of these, however, is to specify a particular noun, to make clear that reference is being made to a particular singular or plural noun. The definite article should be used in the following contexts:

• Second mention (either explicit or implicit)

    a. The surface is covered by *a thin oxide film. The film* protects the surface from corrosion.

    b. A very lightweight car was developed, but *the vehicle* performed poorly in crash tests.

c. A new computer was purchased to complete the process, but *the hard drive* was damaged.

- Superlatives or ordinals

  a. *The most-controlled therapy* yielded the best results.
  b. *The first studies* were conducted in early 1993.
  c. *The last security conference* was termed a success.

- Specifiers (such as *same, sole, only, chief, principal . . .*)

  a. *The same subjects* were retested at 2-week intervals.
  b. *The only research* previously done in this area yielded mixed results.
  c. *The principal causes* of the disaster have yet to be discovered.

- Shared knowledge or unique reference

  a. *The sun* rises in the east and sets in the west.
  b. *The oxygen balance* in the atmosphere is maintained by photosynthesis.
  c. *The stars* are fueled by fusion reactions.

- *Of*-phrases or other forms of post-modification (but not with first mention of partitive* *of*-phrases such as *a molecule of oxygen, a layer of silicon,* or *a piece of information*)

  a. *The behavior of this species* varies.
  b. *The price of gold* fluctuates.
  c. *The results of the investigation* were inconclusive.

- Partitive *of*-phrases with plurals

  a. *None of the projects* was satisfactory.
  b. *Some of the subjects* had adverse reactions.
  c. *All of the questionnaires* were returned.

---

*A partitive phrase is a construction which denotes part of a whole.

- Names of theories, effects, devices, scales, and so on, modified by a proper name used as an adjective

    a. *the Doppler* effect
    b. *the Heisenberg* uncertainty principle
    c. *the Hubble* telescope
    d. *the Kelvin* scale

Note, however, that when a proper name is used in possessive form, no article is used.

    a. Coulomb's law
    b. Einstein's theory of relativity
    c. Broca's area
    d. Wegener's hypothesis

4. Acronyms and Abbreviations

Acronyms and abbreviations follow the same rules as nouns that are spelled out. Review the guidelines in sections 1 through 3 and then look at the following examples.

a/an/∅

This device contains *an LED*.*
   (Note the use of *an*. As with other nouns, if the first *sound* is a vowel sound, then *an* is used.)
A TFT was used.
This computer has *a CD ROM*.
R&D is a high priority.
NASA is working on a space station.

---

*LED = light emitting diode, TFT = thin film transmitter, CD = compact disc, ROM = read only memory, R&D = research and development, NASA = National Aeronautics and Space Administration.

the

Taxes in *the EC** are relatively high.
Some of *the LEDs* need to be replaced.
The LCD in this computer is of high quality.
The GNP of the United States has fluctuated greatly.
It is difficult to say which is *the best PC*.

Notice that when acronyms and abbreviations are used as modifiers, you should focus on the head noun as you choose your article.

An EC response to this situation can be expected.
Many items had to be removed from *the NASA budget* submitted
earlier this year.
A new R&D initiative was outlined by the president.

Task Two

Read this passage on writing and then fill in the blank with either *a*,
an, *the*, or ∅.

_____ writing is _____ complex sociocognitive

process involving _____ construction of _____

recorded messages on _____ paper or some other mate-

rial and, more recently, on _____ computer screen.

_____ skills needed to write range from making

_____ appropriate graphic marks, through utilizing

_____ resources of _____ chosen language, to

anticipating _____ reactions of _____ in-

---

*EC = European Community, LCD = liquid crystal display, GNP = gross national
product, PC = personal computer.

tended readers. _____ writing as composing needs to be distinguished from _____ simpler task of _____ copying. _____ writing is slower than _____ other skills of _____ listening, _____ reading, and _____ speaking. It is further slowed by _____ processes of _____ thinking, _____ rereading what has been written, and _____ revising. _____ writing is not _____ natural ability like _____ speaking, but has to be acquired through _____ years of _____ training or _____ schooling. Although _____ writing systems have been in existence for about 5,000 years, even today, only _____ minority of _____ world's population knows how to write.

Task Three

Read this passage on hearing aids and then fill in the blanks with either *a, an, the,* or ∅.

As _____ average population of _____ United States has increased, so too has _____ number of _____ hearing impaired individuals. Approximately _____ 20 million hearing aids are now in use, and this number is expected to rise. Although there have been _____ considerable advances in _____ hearing aid technology, they still have _____ number of _____ drawbacks, one of _____ most notable ones being problems in dealing with ＿＿＿＿＿＿ important

environmental sounds. For example, ＿＿＿＿＿＿ people who

are deaf in both ears are unable to determine ＿＿＿＿＿＿

direction of ＿＿＿＿＿＿ sound with ＿＿＿＿＿＿ conven-

tional hearing aid. This limitation could result in ＿＿＿＿＿＿

accident or injury if ＿＿＿＿＿＿ wearer cannot decide

＿＿＿＿＿＿ direction of ＿＿＿＿＿＿ siren or

＿＿＿＿＿＿ other warning sound. ＿＿＿＿＿＿ Another

problem concerns ＿＿＿＿＿＿ people suffering from

＿＿＿＿＿＿ high-frequency hearing loss. This type of

＿＿＿＿＿＿ hearing loss removes many consonants and other

useful environmental noises, such as ＿＿＿＿＿＿ ringing of

＿＿＿＿＿＿ telephone.

Task Four

Now, edit the rest of the passage on hearing aids, inserting articles
with a caret (∧) as necessary. The first sentence has been done for
you.

To overcome these limitations, researchers have been investigating ∧ possibility of multiprogrammable hearing device that
    the
could perform two functions. One would be to convert high-
frequency information to low frequencies that fall in range of
normal hearing. Other would involve producing LED display that
could indicate probable direction of sound. Since same device can
perform two functions, it could be used by wider range of consumers than conventional devices. Prototypes of device are cur-

rently being tested. If successful, it should be commercially available within next five years.

5. Generics

So far, we have only discussed article use for specific nouns. Generic nouns, however, are equally important. Generics are as important as specific nouns for academic writing because

1. they more frequently occur in highly formal English;
2. they are more likely to occur in introductions and conclusions, because they are closely associated with generalizations (often of an abstract nature);
3. they are often associated (when they occur) with initial (and topic) sentences in paragraphs; and
4. they tend to occur in the subject position in sentences (either as the subject or following *of*-phrases).

Generic versus Specific Nouns

A generic noun or noun phrase can represent an entire class or can be one representative of a class of objects, people, quantities, or ideas. A generic noun is like an archetype in that it manifests what is typical for the class. For this reason, generics are used in formal definitions (see Unit Two.) Compare the specific and generic noun phrases in table 25.

The specific noun phrases refer to something real. The generic noun phrases, on the other hand, refer to either an entire class or a representative of the class. You may have noticed in table 25 that there are different types of generic noun phrases. Can you describe the differences?

Abstract versus Concrete Generics

Generics can generally be divided into two different types: the abstract generic and the concrete generic. An abstract generic refers to *an entire class* of objects, while the concrete generic refers to a *representative* of a class. Look at the examples in table 26.

TABLE 25. Specific versus Generic Noun Phrases

Specific	Generic
The disinfectant caused an allergic reaction.	*A disinfectant* is an agent capable of destroying disease causing microorganisms.
The solar car engineered at the University of Michigan won the race.	*A solar* car would certainly result in a cleaner atmosphere.
The computer crashed in the middle of the program.	*The computer* has replaced *the typewriter.*
The trees in this region have suffered from the drought.	*Trees* are valuable in maintaining air quality.
Add *some water* to the solution.	*Water* is essential for all living beings.

TABLE 26. Abstract Generic versus Concrete Generic

Abstract generic: the entire class	Concrete generic: a representative of the class
The wasp can detect unique volatile compounds over great distances.	*A wasp* can be trained to detect odors.
The laser has a great many uses in medicine.	*A laser* can be used by *a surgeon* to make very clean cuts.
The computer has been invaluable in scientific advancement.	*Computers* are playing a growing role in all aspects of university life.
—	*Concrete* is relatively cheap.

Abstract generics require *the*, while concrete generics use either *a* (with a singular countable noun) or ∅ (for plural countables and uncountable nouns).

In each of the examples in table 26, a generalization is being made. The abstract generics refer to the entire class. Singular concrete generics, on the other hand, refer to a generalized instance of the class. Finally, plural concrete generics and uncountable generics do not allow for such a clear distinction between class and representative. They can, however, be used when referring to a generalized instance.

Verb Tenses with Generic Nouns

Because generics are used to make generalized statements, they are typically used only with the simple tenses, particularly the present. Nevertheless, they can sometimes be used with the present perfect or the continuous.

The elephant *has come* dangerously close to extinction.
Synthetic skin *is replacing* animals in the testing of cosmetic products.

These examples present a changing, not yet fully realized, situation. In this context, the use of the present perfect or the continuous is appropriate.

Choosing the Proper Generic Form

Given that there are many possible generic forms, how do you know which to use? Should you use an abstract or a concrete generic? Singular or plural? Although there is no absolute rule for your choice, there is a tendency in academic writing to use the abstract generic (*the* + a singular noun) more often than the concrete. Even so, generic use will often depend on your field of study and on the type of noun you are using.

In medicine and biology, generics are common: abstract reference is made to *the heart*, *the liver*, *the brain*, and other parts of the body. On the other hand, in medical English, the names of diseases tend *not* to involve generics, except for colloquialisms like *the flu*. In the sciences and engineering, plural concrete generic reference and $\emptyset$-article concrete generics are common in many contexts. Hence, we see *lasers, quantum wells, bonds, atoms,* and *combustion, catalysis, ionization,* etc. The abstract generic is mainly used with instruments and devices.

The optical scanner is in widespread use.

You should become familiar with the use of generics in your own field of study. By looking through some journal articles, you can begin to get a sense of how things are done in your field.

Generic noun phrases do not follow the same rules for article use as specific nouns do. It is sometimes possible to shift from $\emptyset$ to *a* with generics and vice versa. However, it is not possible to shift from $\emptyset$ to *the* or from *a* to *the.*

Task Five

Read this passage and fill in the blanks with either *a, an, the,* or $\emptyset$.

Much has been learned about _____ brain in

_____ last 150 years. _____ brain,

_____ most complicated organ of _____ body,

contains _____ ten billion nerve cells and is divided

into _____ two cerebral hemispheres—one on

_____ right and one on _____ left. In-

terestingly, _____ left hemisphere controls

_____ movements on _____ right side of

_____ body, while _____ right hemisphere

controls _____ movements on _____ left.

_____ researchers also know that _____

specific abilities and behaviors are localized; in _____

other words, they are controlled by _____ specific areas of _____ brain. _____ language, it seems, is highly localized in _____ left hemisphere. In _____ 1860s Dr. Paul Broca discovered that _____ damage to _____ front left part of _____ brain resulted in _____ telegraphic speech similar to that of young children. Soon thereafter, Karl Wernicke found that _____ damage to _____ back left part of _____ brain, resulted in _____ speech with _____ little semantic meaning. These two regions in _____ brain are now referred to as _____ Broca's area and _____ Wernicke's area.

Although there is some debate surrounding _____ specialization of _____ brain, _____ researchers generally agree that _____ speech is controlled by _____ left side. There is no debate that in _____ great majority of cases, _____ injuries to _____ left side nearly always have _____ impact on _____ speech.

Appendix Two
Academic English and Latin Phrases

Nearly all academic languages make occasional use of foreign phrases and expressions, either to add technical precision or to add "color" to the text. English is no exception. Although in many fields the use of expressions or words from French or German may be declining in academic English, the tradition of incorporating bits of Latin remains surprisingly strong. For that reason, this appendix (*appendix* is a Latin word!) deals only with Latin. We include this appendix primarily to help you negotiate Latin expressions in your reading. You should consider the preferences of your field when deciding whether to use such expressions in your own writing.

Did you know that *per* in *percent* or *kilometers per hour* is a Latin preposition that originally meant *through* or *by*? *Per* is also used in the Latin expression *per se* meaning *through or of itself*, and hence "intrinsically."

Although education conveys important economic benefits, it is also valuable *per se*.

As this example shows, Latin expressions are often set apart from the English language text by italics.

Did you know that all the following abbreviations derive from Latin? How many do you know? How many can you give the full form for?

1. e.g.
2. i.e.
3. N.B.
4. A.M.
5. P.M.
6. P.S.
7. etc.
8. A.D.

We have divided this appendix into three sections.

1. Expressions Referring to Textual Matters

There are quite a number of these, which we display in table 27.

TABLE 27. Common Latin Expressions

Expression	Full form	Literal meaning	Modern use
cf.	*confer*	compare	compare
e.g.	*exempli gratia*	free example	for example
et al.	*et alii*	and others	and other authors
etc.	*et cetera*	and others	and others
errata	*errata*	errors	list of typographical mistakes
ibid.	*ibidem*	in the same place	the same as the previous reference
i.e.	*id est*	that is	that is to say
infra	*infra*	below	see below
loc. cit.	*loco citato*	in the place cited	in the place cited
N.B.	*nota bene*	note well	take note
op. cit.	*opere citato*	in the work cited	in the work cited
passim	*passim*	here and there	the point is made in several places
P.S.	*post scriptum*	after writing	something added after the signature
sic	*sic*	thus	the error is in the original quote
supra	*supra*	above	see above
viz.	*videlicet*	obviously	namely

2. Latin Expressions Starting with a Preposition

a fortiori	with even stronger reason
a posteriori	reasoning based on past experience, or from effects to causes

a priori	deductive reasoning, or from causes to effects
ab initio	from the beginning
ad hoc	improvised, for a specific occasion, not based on regular principles (e.g., an *ad hoc* solution.)
ad infinitum	to infinity, so for forever or without end
ad lib	at will, so to speak off the top of the head
ante meridiem	before noon, typically abbreviated A.M.
antebellum	before the war, usually before the American Civil War
circa (c. or ca.)	about, approximately, usually used with dates (e.g., c. 500 A.D.)
de facto	from the fact, so existing by fact, not by right (e.g., in a *de facto* government)
de jure	from the law, so existing by right
ex post facto	after the fact, so retrospectively
in memoriam	in the memory of a person
in situ	in its original or appointed place (e.g., research conducted *in situ*)
in toto	in its entirety
in vitro	in a glass (e.g., experiments conducted *in vitro*)
in vivo	in life, experiments conducted on living organisms
inter alia	among other things
per capita	per head (e.g., a *per capita* income of $20,000)
per diem	per day (e.g., expenses allowed each day)
post meridiem	after noon, usually abbreviated to P.M.
postmortem	after death, an examination into the cause of death
pro rata	in proportion (e.g., *pro rata* payment for working half time)
sine die	without a day, with no time fixed for the next meeting
sine qua non	without which not, hence an essential precondition for something.

3. Other Expressions

anno Domini (A.D.)	in the year of the Lord, or the number of years after the beginning of Christianity
bona fide	in good faith (e.g., a *bona fide* effort to solve a problem)
caveat	a caution or warning (e.g., *Caveat emptor*, "let the buyer beware")
ceteris paribus	other things being equal (much used by economists)
curriculum vitae	a statement in note form of a person's achievements
ego	literally "I," the consciousness or projection of oneself
locus classicus	the standard or most authoritative source of an idea or reference
quid pro quo	something for something, to give or ask for something in return for a favor or service
status quo	things as they are, the normal or standard situation
viva (voce)	an oral examination

There are further uses of Latin that this appendix does not cover. Most obviously, it does not deal with the technical details of Latin names in the life sciences. However, we observe, in passing, that Latin names do not take generic articles (see Appendix One). Compare:

The Common Loon breeds in the northern part of Michigan.
Gavia immer breeds in the northern part of Michigan.

Finally, this appendix does not address the widespread use of Latin in British and American law.

Appendix Three
Electronic Mail

Electronic mail (or E-mail) is a relatively new way of exchanging messages via computer. Since increasing numbers of graduate students have access to E-mail facilities, the purpose of this appendix is to offer some suggestions about E-mail communications for non-native speakers. These guidelines are primarily for messages that you might send to people you do not know well or to people of higher status, such as advisors or instructors. Messages to friends are your own personal business. These suggestions deal with matters of "etiquette," not with how to actually use E-mail (for example, how to sign on and off).

1. Respond to All Personal Messages Promptly

It is important to let the sender know that you have received an E-mail message sent to you. If you have nothing to reply, at least acknowledge the message. Here are some examples.

Thanks for your query. I will get back to you ASAP.
I've read your message about applying for a fellowship.
Thanks very much for the suggestion. I am thinking about it.
   More soon.
(Do you know what ASAP means? FYI? BTW? If not, see the key at the end of this Appendix)

2. Be Careful about Forwarding Personal Messages

Remember that personal E-mail messages have been sent to you—with you as all or part of the intended audience. Before forwarding a message to somebody else, ask yourself whether the sender would approve. If in doubt, do not.

3. Check Outgoing Messages before Posting Them

Once an E-mail message is sent, it is gone. You cannot get it back. Therefore, read through all the messages you write before sending them. If you think the tone is wrong (too critical, too direct, too apologetic, too feeble, etc.), destroy the message and start again.

Suppose your advisor sends you this message:

> Please have a look at the Mills et al. paper in the latest issue of JACL. I suspect it may be relevant to your project. What do you think?

Why might you decide to *destroy* the following replies? (Remember that *positioning* also applies to E-mail—you want to present yourself as a credible graduate student/junior member of the club.)

a. I have read the Mills paper, but I cannot understand it. Could you please help me by explaining what you had in mind? I'm sorry to be so hopeless.
b. I spent three hours in the library reading and rereading the Mills paper you told me to read. Since it deals with wheat and my project concerns corn, I fail to see how it is relevant in any way. Sincerely
c. Thanks for the wonderful suggestion to read the paper by Mills et al. I have just finished reading it and am changing my project completely. I realize that you are a busy person, but I would like to see you tomorrow to get some more of your advice.

If you are unsure why you might want to destroy these replies, please see the key at the end of this Appendix.

4. Use the Subject Line to Indicate the Topic

Especially in sequences of E-mail messages, subject lines help receivers to recognize the topic (rather than making them search their memories). They also help to make the messages concise and precise. In the following message, notice how the student cleverly uses the subject line to avoid repeating herself.

Message 20741953, 10 lines
Posted: 4:15 EST, Tue Mar 9/93
Subject: Guest Speaker for ED 817 "Int. & Comp. Ed"
To: Joan Robinson
From: Sally Madison

How would you like to be one? Professor Walsh is looking for
someone to spend an hour with our tiny seminar (about 8
people), and I suggested you . . . The class meets on Tuesdays
from 4–7. Let me know your inclination! Thanks, Sally

5. Do Not Overuse Conversational Openings and Closings

As we can see from the examples already given, E-mail language is a
hybrid of speech and writing. Because of its speech elements, many
international students tend to use conversational openings and clos-
ings from (phone) conversations. We often see messages that open
and close like this:

Hi Chris! How are you? This is Fatima from your 321 class. Can I
change the time for our appointment until Friday? I have a test on
Wednesday. Have a good day. Got to run. Bye, bye. Fatima.

At first, recipients may find these conversational messages charm-
ing and appealing. However, over the longer run, you are likely to
come across as unbusinesslike and somewhat naive.

Notice, too, that in many cases E-mail allows you to avoid the
problem of determining how to address someone. You do not have to
choose among such greetings as the following:

Dear Dr. Smith
Dr. Roger Smith
Dear Roger Smith   I'm afraid I will be ten minutes late to-
Dear Roger   day.
Dear Doctor
Dear Advisor

6. Express "Business" Requests Politely

E-mail language is typically informal. In many ways, this feature is very helpful for nonnative speakers. It helps to build relationships. It also allows people to use the system quickly and without worrying too much about *typos*, imperfect sentences, and so on. There is, however, one situation where this informality can be very problematic. When a student sends a request to a faculty member or an administrator, informal language may be too direct and thus insufficiently polite. Two examples follow. The first might be considered only a little offensive, the second rather more so. Of course, giving offense was not the intention of either writer:

Message 21007255, Reply to: 20529115, 8 lines
Posted: 11:12 EST, Tue Aug 3/94
Subject: Pages
To: Joan Robinson
From: Keiko Ichiko

Dear Professor Robinson,

Finally, I can give you something to read. I will leave it in your mailbox soon, so please pick it up when you stop by.

This first message is problematic for two reasons. First, there is the vagueness of *soon*. (How many times will Professor Robinson have to check her mailbox before she finds Keiko's pages?) Second, the end of the message is completely unnecessary. Here is a simple "repair":

Dear Professor Robinson,
Finally, I can give you something to read. I will leave it in your mailbox by noon tomorrow.

Here is the second example.

Message: 20899310, 4 lines
Posted: 12:19 EST, Sun Aug 29/93
Subject: Paper
To: Henry Rabkin
From: Kumar Bhatia

> I am currently working on a paper (approx 8/9 pages). I should
> be done on Mon. evening. Could you please go through it & give
> your comments by Wed.

Studies of politeness suggest three elements for polite requests:

1. Do not impose.
2. Give options.
3. Make the receiver feel good.

Notice how Kumar breaks all three rules. Here is what he might
have written instead.

> I am currently working on a paper (approx 8/9 pages). I should be
> done on Mon. evening. If you are not too busy, I would appreciate
> any comments you might have to make before I submit it. Unfor-
> tunately, it is due on Wed., so there isn't much time. If you can
> help, I'll bring you my draft as soon as it's done. If you can't, that's
> quite OK too.

In contrast, here is a superb student request that John received.

> Message: 20152880, 4 lines
> Posted: 5:32 EST, Thu Feb 18/93
> Subject: Article review
> To: John Swales
> From: Rita Simpson
>
> I was wondering if you have an article that you want me to re-
> view yet. If you have something appropriate, next week would
> be a good time to get started on it. Don't want to sound anxious
> to get going on this, but I'll be around, so let me know. Thanks.

It is clear that Rita really wants to get going on this assignment,
and perhaps believes that John has been a little slow off the mark.
However, she presents herself as being very relaxed about it; notice
in particular her use of the past continuous ("I was wondering") to
give distance to her request. This message is a very good example of
how to be informal and polite at the same time. (It was also immediately successful.)

7. Learn common abbreviations

Many terms and expressions are abbreviated in E-mail. For example, among those abbreviations we have used in this appendix are *ASAP* and *Mon*. Notice others as they scroll across your screen.

8. Do Not Worry Too Much about Capitalization

The normal rules for capitalization are often relaxed in E-mail, presumably to avoid the use of the Shift key. Here is an extreme example.

> thanks for your inquiry about the next tesol conf. it's in atlanta from march 16 to 20—the hq hotel is the hilton.

We suggest that you do not go this far. On the other hand, a few people still send all their messages in capital letters, a custom probably picked up from cables and telexes. TODAY MOST PEOPLE FIND MESSAGES IN ALL CAPS rather threatening and imposing. As one of our students commented, it very much seems like shouting. Do not use this convention. But you can use upper case, instead of underlining, for emphasis.

9. Avoid Deletions

It is becoming usual to leave out certain articles and pronouns and various other bits and pieces of English grammar in E-mail.

Standard English:
> I have read your message about Smith's dissertation. I will return it to your mailbox as soon as possible.

E-mail style:
> Read yr message re smith's diss. will return to yr mailbox ASAP.

Unless your English grammar is very strong, we recommend that you do not use these deletions. You may teach yourself bad habits.

10. Avoid Conventions for Communicating Emotions

E-mail is a written medium but has many of the characteristics of speech. In speech, we can use voice inflection and gesture to communicate what we are feeling. Some E-mail users adopt special symbols to communicate their state of mind: :-) = happy, ˆ0ˆ = worried. Alternatively, they may choose from a small set of special words placed in brackets, and often followed by an exclamation mark. Here is an example:

> Here is an update on my project. I have spent three days running the analysis (phew!), but will need another two days to get it done (sigh). Then I plan to have a break and visit a friend in Chicago for three days (smile!).

These devices are fine to use in E-mail for friends. They also seem more widely used by undergraduates than by graduates. We advise against using them in "business" messages.

A Final Word

In this appendix, we have provided some suggestions for using E-mail. We hope in this way to increase your confidence. We do not want in any way to make you anxious about this means of communication. Many nonnative speakers find E-mail to be an ideal way of communicating. If you have an opportunity to get on a system, enjoy it and learn from it.

Key

ASAP = as soon as possible
FYI = for your information
BTW = by the way

Possible reasons you should destroy the replies include the following:

a. You do indeed seem rather hopeless here. Even if you did not understand the paper, do you need to say so? Like this?
b. You seem rather irritated—and perhaps you missed the point. What if your advisor thinks that it is the methodology part that is relevant? Perhaps it would be wiser to respond with a question like this: "Could you be more specific about which parts of the paper are most relevant?"
c. You sound like you cannot think for yourself and are too eager to please your advisor.

Selected References

Since this book is a guide to writing academic English, many of the illustrative texts contain citations. For obvious reasons, we have not included these illustrative citations in this reference list. Instead, we have chosen to include only citations of work in our own field (studies of academic English and how to write it).

Every publisher requires its authors to use a particular style for references. The University of Michigan Press follows the *Chicago Manual of Style*. Other book and journal publishers may use other styles that may vary from the Chicago manual in minor or major ways.

Bavelas, J. B. 1978. The social psychology of citations. *Canadian Psychological Review* 19:158–63.

Becher, T. 1987. Disciplinary discourse. *Studies in Higher Education* 12:261–74.

Cooper, C. 1985. Aspects of article introductions in IEEE publications. M.Sc. Thesis, Aston University, U.K.

Gilbert, G. N. 1977. Referencing and persuasion. *Social Studies of Science* 7:113–22.

Graetz, N. 1985. Teaching EFL students to extract structural information from abstracts. In *Reading for Professional Purposes*, edited by J. M. Ulijn and A. K. Pugh, 123–35. Leuven, Belgium: ACCO.

Hoey, M. 1983. *On the surface of discourse*. London: Allen and Unwin.

Huckin, T. 1987. Surprise value in scientific discourse. Paper presented at the CCC Convention, Atlanta.

Knorr-Cetina, K. D. 1981. *The manufacture of knowledge*. Oxford: Pergamon.

Master, P. 1986. *Science, medicine, and technology: English grammar and technical writing*. Englewood Cliffs, N.J.: Prentice Hall.

Moravcsik, M. J. 1985. *Strengthening the coverage of third world science*. Eugene, Oreg.: Institute of Theoretical Science.

Olsen, L. A., and T. N. Huckin 1990. Point-driven understanding in engineering lecture comprehension. *English for Specific Purposes* 9:33–48.

Ravetz, J. R. 1971. *Scientific knowledge and social problems*. Oxford: Oxford University Press.

Skelton, J. 1988. The care and maintenance of hedges. *English Language Teaching Journal* 42:37–44.

St. John, M. J. 1987. Writing processes of Spanish scientists publishing in English. *English for Specific Purposes* 6:113–20.

Swales, J. M. 1990. *Genre analysis: English in academic and research settings*. Cambridge: Cambridge University Press.

Swales, J. M., and H. Najjar. 1987. The writing of research article introductions. *Written Communication* 4:175–92.

Tarone, E., S. Dwyer, S. Gillette, and V. Icke. 1981. On the use of the passive in two astrophysical journal papers. *English for Specific Purposes* 1: 123–40.

Thompson, D. K. 1993. Arguing for experimental "facts" in science: A study of research article Results sections in biochemistry. *Written Communication* 8:106–28.

Weissberg, R., and S. Buker. 1990. *Writing up research: Experimental research report writing for students of English*. Englewood Cliffs, N.J.: Prentice Hall.

Task One

There are 19 references in our reference list. How many of each of the following types are there?

Scholarly books	_____
Textbooks	_____
Journal articles	_____
Book chapters	_____
Theses and Dissertations	_____
Unpublished papers	_____

Task Two

Based on our reference list, what can you determine about the *Chicago Manual* rules for using capital letters in titles in bibliographies?

Index